Dr. Gil Stieglitz is like a Dr. John Go[t] have seen countless marriages transformed through Dr. Gil's marital wisdom. A healthy marriage is such a powerful witness to Christ's relationship with his bride, the Church. In *Building a Ridiculously Great Marriage*, there is remarkable wisdom that you can test on your marriage. His insights in this book are consistently practical. Try them, and you will see the difference in real time. Dr. Gil has discovered this biblical wisdom over decades of working with healthy and hurting couples. This book is rooted in incarnational reality.

Wouldn't you like your marriage or future marriage to be "ridiculously" great? Wouldn't you like your non-Christian friends and family to be jealous unto salvation about your great marriage? I encourage you to invest in that dream by reading Dr. Gil's latest marriage book. You will not regret taking this step. Better yet, buy a second copy for a friend or family member who could benefit.

— REV. DR. ED HIRD

CO-AUTHOR OF *FOR BETTER, FOR WORSE:*
DISCOVERING THE KEYS TO A LASTING RELATIONSHIP
EDHIRD.COM

The last time you heard the word "ridiculous" in your marriage, it was likely not a good thing. My friend, Gil Stieglitz, will help you redeem the word *ridiculous* and make it GREAT in your marriage. Gil is a teacher, trainer, and personal coach for you and your spouse. Read this book and get the help you need now and for the future. I believe what he teaches here can make your marriage ridiculously great!

— DR. JOHN JACKSON, PRESIDENT OF
WILLIAM JESSUP UNIVERSITY

AUTHOR OF BOOKS ON LEADERSHIP AND TRANSFORMATION
DRJOHNJACKSON.COM

There were times when someone told me, "Do you know Peter and Mary? They just divorced!" My response was sometime like, "Ridiculous! How can that be?" I have been a pastor for thirty-one years, and I have seen too many times how Satan cunningly, tactfully, strategically, and ridiculously destroys a wonderful and good marriage! Now we have Dr. Gil's newest book, *Building a Ridiculously Great Marriage*. Wow! Bravo!

Although Gil says that the fifteen fundamental habits are in no particular order, I so wish that habit #7 "Pray Individually and Together" would be top-priority #1. Why? Because I know all too well that we as human beings cannot win over Satan's well-planned strategy to destroy a marriage on our own. Only when a couple can build up a daily habit and lifestyle to be with Jesus will they have a ridiculously great marriage. I do not think there is another way! Thank you, Dr. Gil, for your new book. I have been using your *Marital Intelligence* book for my couple's group for many years, and now they can have your new book to enjoy and enrich!

— RT. REV. DR. SILAS NG

CHIEF BISHOP, ANGLICAN MISSION IN CANADA

You know what's ridiculous? How many marriages are failing to survive or simply going through the motions without any passion and excitement. None of us ever think that will happen to us. "Our marriage will be different," we say to ourselves, but before we know it we're in a rut, frustrated with our spouse, and the direction we're heading in. That's why this book by Dr. Stieglitz is a must read for any and every married couple. It's not that there aren't thousands of books on marriage on the market, but very few give such helpful and practical advice as this one does. Don't hesitate, pick this book up and start the journey of giving your marriage a shot of adrenaline and a health boost. You won't regret it.

— DR. DAVID FASOLD

LEAD PASTOR, BAY HILLS COMMUNITY CHURCH, RICHMOND, CA

Dr. Gil Stieglitz is a force to be reckoned with. Full of wisdom, insight, and a never-say-die attitude, his love for Christ and people is contagious. In *Building a Ridiculously Great Marriage*, you will receive years of proven tactics with practical application. Each section drips with biblical backing ready to help make any marriage soar. Gil has personally blessed my own marriage in numerous ways, for which my wife and I are forever grateful. He is the real deal, an apostle Paul of our generation who never gives up because he knows just how precious, how valuable, every marriage is in God's eyes. You can take him at his every word, every time.

Do yourself a favor and get your hands on a copy of this book. Immerse yourself in the rich wisdom embedded within its pages, and watch what God does in your and your spouse's relationship. I guarantee, you won't regret it.

— TYLER AND ALLIE SWANEY

HIGH SCHOOL PASTORS, BAYSIDE CHURCH, GRANITE BAY CAMPUS

In 1989, Stephen Covey published a book that changed the way people think about themselves called *The 7 Habits of Highly Effective People*. Thirty years later, Gil Stieglitz has written a book that has purposefully and successfully given clear, practical steps that will change the way people think about marriage!

It's easy to get married. It's not so easy to stay married. The marriage connection is the most sacred relationship we can have on earth with another human being. For over twenty-five years, I have coached, walked through, prayed and cried with hundreds of couples due to issues in their marriage. I have struggled to find a resource that encompasses the steps toward a great marriage...until now. This book is full of practical, creative, proven steps and instructions for couples to work through together.

Imagine a marriage where there is mutual respect, humility, support, service, and trust. You and I can most certainly achieve this! *Building a Ridiculously Great Marriage* should be required reading by everyone before AND after they get married.

— DAN CHRYSTAL

AUTHOR OF *THE LOST ART OF RELATIONSHIP: A JOURNEY TO FIND THE LOST COMMANDMENT*
LOSTARTBOOK.COM
HUSBAND, FATHER, PASTOR, SPEAKER, COACH, THRIVER

In a time where most marriages are barely surviving, Dr. Gil Stieglitz writes *Building a Ridiculously Great Marriage* to encourage, equip, and motivate couples to build healthy habits and practices that will help them thrive in all aspects of their relationship. Dr. Gil writes honestly, logically, and practically by equipping couples with tools and resources to build that ridiculously great marriage foundation every couple seeks to find. This book is written for all seasons, circumstances, and challenges that couples experience in their lifetime. Dr. Gil's marriage research and extensive work with couples has impacted thousands of marriages around the globe—I would love for your marriage to be one of them!

— LISA THOMPSON

WOMEN'S PASTOR, BAYSIDE CHURCH, GRANITE BAY, CA
AUTHOR OF *FAITH JOURNEY BIBLE STUDIES*

✤ ALSO BY GIL STIEGLITZ ✤

BUILDING A Ridiculously GREAT MARRIAGE

GIL STIEGLITZ

PTLB
PRINCIPLES
TO LIVE BY
LIFE IS RELATIONSHIPS

Building a Ridiculously Great Marriage — Premarital and Marital Habits
© 2019 by Gil Stieglitz

Published by Principles To Live By, P.O. Box 214, Roseville CA 95661.
For more information about this book and the author, visit www.ptlb.com.

Cover Design by:
Dave Eaton

Copyedited by:
Jennifer Edwards
jedwardsediting.net

Book Design by:
Linné Garrett
829DESIGN.COM

Paperback ISBN: 978-0-9968855-8-4
eBook ISBN: 978-0-9909640-7-0
Audible ISBN: 978-0-9909640-8-7

Library of Congress Control Number: 2019915745

REL012050 RELIGION / CHRISTIAN LIVING / LOVE & MARRIAGE
REL012030 RELIGION / CHRISTIAN LIVING / FAMILY & RELATIONSHIPS
REL074000 RELIGION / CHRISTIAN MINISTRY / PASTORAL RESOURCES

Unless otherwise indicated, all Scripture quotations are taken from the NEW AMERICAN STANDARD BIBLE®, Copyright © 1960,1962,1963,1968,1971,1972,1973,1975,1977, 1995 by The Lockman Foundation. Used by permission.

Scripture quotations marked NIV are taken from THE HOLY BIBLE, NEW INTERNATIONAL VERSION®, NIV® Copyright © 1973, 1978, 1984, 2011 by Biblica, Inc.® Used by permission. All rights reserved worldwide.

Scripture quotations marked NLT are taken from the Holy Bible, New Living Translation, copyright © 1996, 2004, 2015 by Tyndale House Foundation. Used by permission of Tyndale House Publishers, Inc., Carol Stream, Illinois 60188. All rights reserved.

PRINTED IN THE UNITED STATES OF AMERICA

☼ Dedication ☼

This book is dedicated to my incredible wife,
DANA STIEGLITZ,
with whom I enjoy a ridiculously great marriage.

You are such a delightful and amazing person, and
I am so deeply in love with you.

The joy I have in loving you is boundless.
Every day, I am excited to wake up with the opportunity
to love you and be loved by you.

Contents

Introduction

RECENTLY, I HAD THE PRIVILEGE OF HELPING A FEW PREMARITAL COUPLES prepare for their marriages. They had been reading through my book *Marital Intelligence* and they were making significant progress. But as I prayed about the best way to help these couples, it seemed like the Lord was directing me to just spell out what they needed to do. In other words, give them the short and dirty version of what creates a ridiculously great marriage. Let me give you a few examples.

Richard and Charmaine decided to get married because they had strong feelings for each other whenever they spent time together. This was a second marriage for both of them, and they were a little apprehensive about entering into another marriage. As we talked, they recognized that they did not really understand why their first marriages broke up. They were going into this new marriage with all the feelings of the first one but with no new routines, systems, or habits to ensure this one would work. For example, they didn't have a way to talk to each other when they were mad. They hadn't really talked about each other's intimacy needs. They didn't know how to have a financial discussion without a fight. They didn't know how to get ahead of problems, so they were regularly arguing about small things.

Marriage doesn't have to be this way. Couples don't have to reach the point where they view their spouse as the enemy, where one spouse wins and the other loses. They can have a marriage that is so great, other couples will stand up and notice—they might even call it "ridiculous."

Many people assume they will have a good marriage. But what they really want is a marriage that surprises them with delight, love, growth, energy, longing, and connection. This is what I mean by a "ridiculous" marriage—one that constantly surprises and is beyond the norm. You feel like you lucked into this great relationship. I love how when I see my wife, Dana, I am always delighted. Even after all the years we've been married, my heart still jumps. Being with her is delightful, encouraging, deep, helpful, and playful. The sort of connection we have is to die for. I know of many couples who have this type of connection in their marriage, and I have found that the routines, systems, and habits I talk about in this book are present in every one of them. You can have this kind of marriage too if you are serious about putting these tried and true practices to work.

One of my hero couples is Charles and Vi. They have what I would classify as a ridiculously good marriage. Their marriage is a marvelous mix of love, playfulness, wisdom, and hard work. By their own admission, though, it hasn't always been wonderful. Both would admit that the mastermind behind their great marriage is Vi; her wisdom and introduction of these habits into their married life has been instrumental in the way they live today. They learned how to have financial discussions so both of them would feel secure with the decisions they made. Despite both of their busy schedules, they made sure to have a least one meal together every day to talk, debrief, encourage, and recharge. They constantly aligned their expectations to eliminate conflicts. They were consistent with praise and appreciation for one another. They did not take each other for granted. They refused to put the other one down even when they knew the other one had blown it. Over the years, Vi has slowly injected these habits into their married life until this is the way they live. Charles began to embrace these habits slowly as his own and is now enjoying the richness of a ridiculously great marriage.

Too often we think we need to make changes in our marriage through some kind of peace summit, where we both agree to do things this way all the time. No, usually these habits start by one person practicing them until it just becomes the way that "we" are married. In the beginning years of the marriage, Vi was the only one who was doing these habits, and Charles was barely participating. Slowly but surely, these habits pushed out the problems and rough spots in their relationship. It can be this way for your marriage, too.

Every successful person in any arena of life has little habits they do that others do not do. It is these little habits that push them to the front of the pack. From business to sports to financial success and marriage, a few key habits will make all the difference. In this book, I introduce fifteen fundamental habits that all great marriages have and are not present in bad ones. It seems like all great couples have some version of these routines, systems, and habits they use. This book is like the cheat sheet to ace the Marriage Test. I will take you through them one habit at a time.

These little routines can change the way couples relate to one another. Even though they may seem a little odd at first, try them, practice them. I think you will find these to be like oil in the engine of your marriage. Everything will go much more smoothly. You will learn how to avoid problems, how to keep your love alive, and how to develop a true companion through the ups and downs of life. I have watched so many marriages go up in flames because the couple doesn't have systems in place to handle conflicts that will come up. They don't practice these invaluable habits because they don't know what they are. They think they won't need these hooky things—they say, "our love is strong enough for any problems." But the fact is that these little routines are what keep the love strong.

If you are a married or engaged couple reading this together, my hope for you is that you will adopt these habits and adjust them to fit your relationship. Some version of these habits needs to show up in your marriage. If you are reading this on your own, I hope you, like Vi, will talk these over with your partner and slowly begin to insert them into your relationship. Don't give up if you get resistance, just keep working on them. Your partner will come around, you'll see.

If you know someone who is about to get married, then pass on these habits to them. The goal for all married couples is to have a marriage filled with joy—one that is complete, unified, and full of mutual love and respect—a ridiculously great marriage. These habits will help them get there.

Now if you have been divorced and are considering marriage again, I hope these routines, systems, and habits will make sense to you and help you identify things that were missing in the previous relationship. May this book help you lay a new foundation for the ridiculously great marriage you deserve.

Debrief Daily

Josh and Sharon were like most other married couples. They had settled into routines they thought were working for them. Little did they know there was one routine they were leaving out that was slowly killing their marriage. Josh would come home every day and plop himself in front of the TV until dinner, then play with the kids, watch some more TV with his wife, and go to bed. Day after day, Sharon watched her husband be a great father and even a great provider who was faithful to her, but she was slowly losing touch with him. She had no idea what he was thinking, what he was going through, or even what he did all day. And he certainly didn't know anything about her thoughts, feelings, or daily challenges, either.

It finally reached a climax about ten years into the marriage when Sharon couldn't take being ignored anymore. She packed up the kids and left; she didn't know why she was so depressed and unable to soldier on anymore but she just couldn't. Josh came home to find his house empty with no warning or understanding of what was happening. He came to my office for help, and after we sorted through all that had taken place, I figured out the problem. They didn't have a daily time to talk about what happened to each of them during their day, along with the crucial commentary about what each one thought and felt regarding what they experienced. It was no wonder Sharon left. I counseled Josh to insert a daily debrief into their marriage to take place as soon as he came home. This thirty to sixty minute talk each night connected he and Sharon and allowed both of them to feel heard and valued. It was a win-win for both of them.

Taking time to debrief your day with your spouse is one of the consistent, essential qualities great couples do. Knowing you will be heard every day about the difficulties, victories, and irritations you faced knits a couple together. It sounds bizarre but this simple habit protects the marriage and injects love deep into the marrow of the relationship. Sometimes this can be done over the phone because of travel schedules, but usually it is a face-to-face interaction consisting of a run-down of the people, problems, and feelings of the day. When I was growing up watching my parents do this, it took place as soon as my father got home from work. He and mom went into the back bedroom to talk. They would emerge thirty to sixty minutes later with a renewed sense of understanding and support of one another. They were unified and filled up from their time of talking and sharing. I knew from just looking at them that this habit was a good thing.

INS AND OUTS OF THE DAILY DEBRIEF

The daily debrief is really an intentional, active habit that requires talking, asking questions, and listening. It is a focused time of drawing details out of the other person's day and hearing about how it went. After an extended period of time of not being together all day, the debrief is your chance as a couple to come back together, get on the same page in each other's lives, and move forward with the rest of the evening. It reestablishes the connection. To debrief effectively, it is important to give enough detail and color about your day so the other person can feel they were present with you as you went along. This can be done in a few different ways—chronologically, sharing highlights, or relationally. It will depend on the person as to which type of debriefing is valuable to them, but the other spouse can use the other types to guide the discussion and draw out more details of the day.

Debriefing Chronologically

As you might have guessed, a chronological debrief is a download of the day's events from morning until present in chronological order. Ask your spouse what happened in their day from beginning to end without leaving anything out. Draw them out with questions like:

How did you sleep the night before?

How was your breakfast? What did you eat? Did you think about anything in particular during breakfast? Were you especially excited about the day for any reason?

How was your commute?

What happened during the morning?

Did you get your normal lunch, or was it different?

Did you have any interesting conversations with colleagues, neighbors, or friends?

What was the afternoon like? What did you do? Were you intrigued with anything that happened? Were you discouraged by anything that afternoon? Did you have any good conversations or meetings with people?

When did you shut off and start heading home?

How was the commute on the way home?

I think you get the idea of the depth of sharing I'm talking about here. Once one spouse shares their day, then the other spouse does the same thing—the other one asks questions and listens intently. Of course they won't necessarily be the same questions. If one spouse stays home with the children or works at home, tailor the questions for that. To remain friends and lovers, you must give the gift of listening to what has been happening to your spouse. If you are not willing to listen, you are at risk of objectifying each other as a paycheck or a sexual object or a nanny. Push into being your spouse's friend by listening daily.

Debriefing Highlights

Another way to do a daily debrief is to ask your spouse to share the highlights of their day in any order as they remember them. This will usually be an emotional reordering of the day as people tend to remember and recount the most emotional parts of the day, both good and bad. It is crucial for the listening spouse to ask questions about what the other one is recounting because whatever they say is what they want you to know about them for that day.

It begins with a statement like, "Tell me about your day." Don't assume your spouse will start talking just because this is the time to debrief. Someone has to get it started; that's why it's important to ask every day. When your spouse begins telling you something from the middle of the day, you can assume they are giving you an emotional recap. This means it is emotionally significant to them. Ask questions or make statements to guide their talking, and try to comment and respond to the things they are saying to let them know you are listening, like:

How did that feel when that happened?

You must have been so excited when you heard.

That must have been depressing.

What did you do when they said that?

> *What else happened today?*
>
> *Oh, that must have hurt.*
>
> *I am stunned that happened to you.*
>
> *Oh wow, congratulations, that is wonderful!*
>
> *Amazing, I am so excited for you!*

The idea is to be curious about what they've been through and to emote with them as if you were also there. Your marriage will be stronger when you and your spouse feel heard and understood. This thirty to sixty minutes spent every day talking will accomplish a crucial bonding element.

Debriefing Relationally

A third way to debrief daily is to find out how the relationships in each spouse's life are going. Begin to ask questions about the ten relationships in life (God, self, marriage, family, work, finances, church, friends, society, enemies) until it becomes clear which relationship you want to talk about. Usually, a person prefers one or two of the relationships more than the others. These may be the relationships that are troubling them or ones where they had significant joys or excitement. Many times, your spouse will surprise you with the depth of emotion they are experiencing in one of the non-obvious relationships. Be mindful of any issues in their relationships. Then ask how that area is going and guide the discussion with gentle probing questions, like:

> *How did it go with the kids today?*
>
> *What happened at work today?*
>
> *What are you reading in Scripture?*
>
> *Did you hear what the president said (or what the governor did) today?*
>
> *Did you get any time with Steve or Jarod (friends) today?*
>
> *How was your workout (or your class)?*
>
> *Do you have any thoughts about our vacation plans today?*
>
> *What do you think would be great if we bought/did?*
>
> *How did that message at church last week strike you?*

You will have different ways of asking about these relationships but realize you will probably not hear what your spouse is thinking or feeling about an area if you don't ask. If they don't want to talk about it, they will tell you; or if nothing is relevant to them in that area, there won't be anything that comes up.

As I mentioned above, the actual debriefing and asking questions are only part of the equation. Listening well is the other part. Not many people are adept at listening well, so allow me to share a few listening techniques with you.

LISTENING SKILLS

Listening well is a skill that requires focus and concentration. There will be lots of topics and issues brought up, so can you listen in a way your spouse feels heard? Many people don't know how to listen actively—it isn't something we've been taught unless you're a counselor or a pastor or perhaps a teacher. The thing you need to know is to follow each topic or issue with rapt attention by employing several listening and clarifying techniques. The goal is to make sure your spouse feels heard.

1. *Minimal encouragers*—These provide verbal or nonverbal feedback or cues that signal you are listening. These signals can be a tilted head, a raised eyebrow, a nodding head, or leaning toward the person talking. Much of the time we tell people to keep talking by using little words, phrases, or noises. I have heard people say "well" or "really" as filler words. My mother used the word "no" with different inflections to let you know you had her attention. Some people say "I hear you" or "uh-huh." Some grunt or moan knowingly like they understand what you're saying. If you make no sound at all, it doesn't give the other person any indication you are listening; in fact, it communicates you want them to stop talking, so they will. The goal is to encourage them to keep going, so use minimal encouragers throughout the debrief.

2. *Asking questions*—Ask about what the other person says and draw them out, even though you may not really care about the topic they are talking about. As you can see from the questions above, this is a crucial element in the daily debrief. It says, "I am listening, and I want you to tell me more." When you start asking questions about your spouse's day, you may really struggle to know what to ask, but you will get better, especially as you get familiar with the subject matter, like their job or a topic that matters to them. Remember the real reason you are asking questions is to say to your spouse, "Tell me more." You are communicating to them, "If it is interesting to you, it is interesting to me."

   I find as a marriage counselor, this idea of constant curiosity is an overlooked, crucial element in love and a great marriage. Asking questions says, "I am interested in what you think and feel." One of the rules I give premarital and newlywed couples is to ask at least one question about each item, person, or topic their spouse brings up. There is more to this issue, so you asking at least one question will begin to bring it out. This says "I love you" as few ways can.

One of the things that sustains my marriage is writing down questions that occur to me over the course of the day to ask my wife later. I will read an article, and I'll write down a question about it. I sometimes send the article to her and ask what she thinks about it. Just the other day, I sent her articles about diseases that were emerging from homeless camps and research being done on sharks. These are random ideas, but it lets me know what she thinks and connects us.

One of the other ways many couples use to stay connected is through books of questions or using apps with questions in them. I recommend the Gottman Cards App as a source of good questions. When I am traveling, I stop by those book racks at the airport and look for the books with questions in them. I will throw these in the glove box of the car when I get back so we always have questions to ask each other if the normal conversation gets too boring or same-old-same-old stuff.

Ask questions of your spouse. There is a wealth of ideas, thoughts, feelings, and dreams waiting to be explored. They don't all have to be mined, but it makes for a richer marriage if these things are explored in a helpful, curious conversation.

3. *Paraphrasing*—Restate what the other person is saying so you can reflect back what you are hearing. One of the best ways you can tell your spouse your are listening is to paraphrase back what you thought they were saying. Your partner will tell you if you have the gist of it or not. There will even be many times when you may accurately reflect back what they said, but they tell you that is not what they said or meant. That means they want to convey different content than you heard. Don't be hung up on the exact words; just keep listening and trying to understand what they are trying to communicate. It will help knit you together as a couple.

4. *Summarizing*—Recap what was said and ask if that is what they meant to say. This is where you interrupt a person after a few topics and you ask them, "Now, I want to get this straight. I heard you say that you were upset about the broken window, you were frustrated by the boys, and energized by the report from the school. Is that right?" Using this tool is always instructive when what I heard is different than what my wife was trying to say.

5. *Don't rush it*—Stay at this every night for thirty to sixty minutes if you can. You might have to start with fifteen minutes and build to sixty minutes. If you are self-focused and really only care about what you are interested in, then this will seem like an eternity. Usually, I find that if you stay curious

about each other's worlds, the time will go by very quickly. These are the secrets to great and loving conversations and relationships. Learn these simple elements.

6. *Focused attention*—You might be thinking to yourself, "How do I listen to someone talk about something I don't care about at all?" It's easy. You listen because you love them, which means that whatever they love or are impacted by will cause you to get out of your own little world into theirs. There is nothing more important than this communication. This focused attention says that you love the other person deeply.

CRUCIAL BENEFITS OF DEBRIEFING

Debriefing daily has many crucial benefits besides just being heard or expressing what you have gone through that day. You benefit, your spouse benefits, and your children benefit because the debrief is a bigger deal than you think. Let's take a look at the benefits of debriefing daily:

1. *Builds a Strong Friendship for Difficult Times*

    It's amazing how this daily listening builds friendship bonds that will carry you through difficult times. The daily debrief allows downloading thoughts and feelings and to express any new ideas or solutions either of you has come up with. When there is something stressful going on, especially with one of the kids, you both have likely thought about it off and on throughout the day. I know one couple with a very troubled son who often makes unwise decisions. When they get together at the end of the day, both spouses will have had various conversations or encounters with him separately, so the daily debrief keeps them both informed and up-to-date about what the other one has heard or experienced, as well as any decisions that were made or instructions given to him. Without this daily debrief, it would be easy for the couple to feel isolated and alone with their thoughts or to feel undermined by what the other spouse is doing. The daily debrief is critical in keeping a couple on the same page and team.

2. *Helps You Stay in Love*

    Another benefit I can't emphasize enough is how this daily habit will help you stay in love with the person you married. This face-to-face conversation will allow you to know all about your spouse's inner world, which is one of the keys to a ridiculously great marriage. The things you learn will allow you to love your spouse at new levels. Knowing you are being heard is priceless. The entrance to each other's inner world creates bonds of friendship, love, and appreciation that cannot be bought at any price.

3. *Provides Security for the Children*

This habit will also say to the kids, "My parents are going to stay together," which is critical to kids of all ages. When our children were really small, Dana and I used to sit on the couch in the living room and have the kids in their bedrooms. They were not allowed to come out until we came and got them. It became clear to the kids that mommy and daddy's relationship was very important. One parenting expert says it's important for the kids to see parents talking and making the marriage relationship a priority. When the kids know that mommy and daddy are staying together, it helps them grow strong emotionally.

DERAILING THE DEBRIEF

Since this is one of the most important habits a couple can employ, it helps to be aware of some of the pitfalls that can hinder effectiveness or derail the debrief time altogether. Knowing what to look for will prepare you in advance. Remember the goal of the debrief is for each spouse to feel heard, not just one day, but every day. Here are some issues that can derail the debrief.

1. *Lack of Energy*

It is critical for both parties to save enough of themselves for this debrief so they can give significant attention to their spouse. It is not okay to give all your energy to other places (like work or the kids) and come home having nothing left for the most important person in front of you. I have sometimes suggested that a person pull over and take a nap before they get home to have enough energy for this debrief time. I have also suggested that whoever is watching the kids take a nap or rest whenever the kids nap or rest, so they have the energy for this debrief time. I think what you will find is feeling heard feels good. Do it enough times, and you will crave it; you may even perk up just anticipating it.

2. *Allowing the Children to Dictate*

Finding a good time and place to debrief can be tricky. For some couples, right before dinner is the worst time because of all the chaos, so it would be better to do it after dinner. Some couples take a walk, others sit on the front porch or couch. You have to do what works for you. I advocate for the time right after one or both spouses get home. I have seen that if a couple commits to this particular time, it sends a very strong message to the kids that the marriage is more important than the children. The kids like and appreciate this message because they instinctively know their world is secure when mom and dad are together.

I realize this can be difficult as you are trying to add it into your schedule; do everything you can to find a time and way every day to do this debrief. Yes, your children and everything else will conspire to try and rob you of that time, but don't let them. Get creative! I know of some parents who do the debrief at sports practices while the kids are on the field. The kids just look over and think, "There are my parents having their daily debrief." They know intuitively this helps their parents stay in love. I do not recommend the kids be present during the debrief. They should know that the debrief is happening. If the children are very young, you can consider it a training exercise to teach them to play quietly while mom and dad have their talking time. You might have to begin with a shorter time at first and add time slowly through this process. Children also benefit from a debrief of their day, but this isn't the time. (I usually find the time for the kids to debrief is best before bed when they are most open to talking anyway, especially in their teen years.)

3. *Criticizing Instead of Debriefing*

Another thing that can derail the daily debrief is to use it to criticize when it should be used to download the day's events. Maybe your spouse starts talking about the things you did or didn't do or things that involve you. This can seem like a personal attack as they start talking about things from their point of view. The natural tendency is to interrupt and start defending yourself, which is where the debrief derails. As your spouse shares more deeply and honestly, they may say things you have to let go of without taking it personally. In other words, you can avoid a derail if you don't take what the other person is saying as a personal attack. Determine in your mind that they are talking and you are listening. They don't need solutions; they just need attentive listening. Yes, they may suggest you should do something different. Just keep listening and keep drawing them out on the various subjects. There will be time for solutions and action, but a daily debrief is often a lifeline to a reality that isn't about solutions; it's about being heard.

I have watched this in so many different couples, where the talking gets out of control. If they will just let the other person talk, things work themselves out. They don't need to respond at all. Listening is the best form of healing.

Remember, the daily debrief is one of the essential habits observed in ridiculously great marriages. It is entirely in your control to have a marriage like this, and this is the place to start. If you are the one reading this, then let it begin with you. Don't just read about it and say, "Yes, that would help us!" Set up the time and do it. Begin tonight.

In the next chapter, I will introduce you to the next habit that will slowly, but powerfully, remake your marriage into a delightful relationship—holding weekly staff meetings.

Hold a Weekly Staff Meeting

———

Do you ever feel you are running harder and harder but not getting ahead? The only way to get ahead of the incredible to-do list that lands on everyone, every marriage, and every family is to have a planning meeting. Every effective organization has meetings to plan what they want to do with the week, month, and year ahead, and your family should be no different. Did you know your family is really a business entity? It's true! Like all businesses, your family has income, expenses, personnel, resources, assets, and so on. Each family also has an organizational structure, whether well-organized or more loosely structured. I think it's safe to say that all successful business owners are well-organized, goal-oriented, and work together to achieve their goals. They are also committed to a pre-determined culture consistent with their values. Successful marriages and families do these things too.

Let me give you an example from a premarital counseling session I had with Nate and his fiancé. At the high point of an argument with his wife, Nate had a critical insight. He blurted out,

"I know why we have so many fights and disagreements. We are not getting together to talk about the week before we are in it. We are trying to figure life out with no plan and no agreement. We have to have a meeting before the week starts or it will only get worse."

I suggested they hold a weekly staff meeting and eliminate a lot of these fights.

Success in business or marriage never comes by accident. It takes focus, good communication, and accountability to see things through. Something always present in a successful business is a weekly staff meeting. In fact, I have never heard of any successful business or company that doesn't have one. Yet I talk to married couples all the time who do not have any kind of staff meeting to make sure they are on the same page with schedules, goals, kids, finances, vacations, friendships, and so on. The most important business you are engaged in is your family business, and if your family business does not work, your life does not work. Even the smallest companies with just a few employees have some sort of regular staff meeting to stay on the same page.

The second habit, then, is to establish and hold regular, weekly staff meetings—this is for you and your spouse only, the owners and managers of your family business. This hour or two spent meeting each week is set aside to specifically discuss key elements of your family business, which will keep things moving forward in the ways you both want. Holding this one meeting each week will make a huge difference because now both people have a focused time to get on the same page about the many issues you face or decisions that need to be made. It's a time to discover what each of you thinks about various issue like what's going on with the finances. Or how you will work through the training and discipline issue with the kids. How do the various schedules mesh or clash this next week? What fun thing can the family look forward to? What are both people expecting will happen, and where do those not align? These are just a few of the things you can talk about. You should give some thought about what other topics you want to bring up on a week-to-week basis and add it to the agenda.

Setting and sticking to a weekly staff meeting helps a marriage in so many ways besides just getting organized. Let's dig into some of these.

1. *Avoiding fights, conflicts, and disunity.*

Many couples fight about finances, schedules, and children because of a lack of communication and disunity. The husband has his ideas for how things should be and the wife has hers. The staff meeting is a vehicle both partners can use to get it all out on the table, eliminating surprises or secrecy about what the other one is thinking. Many couples employ the "I-will-try-to-remember-to-bring-it-up" method of communication, which doesn't work all that well. I don't know about you, but I have so many things swirling around in my head every day; sometimes I forget to mention something that needs to be talked about or there just isn't enough time in the week to thoroughly discuss it. The weekly staff meeting helps with this.

Other times, couples have issues that haven't yet been given the back-and-forth dialogue necessary to develop a unified position. Or they think *now* in the heat of a fight or when the kids are screaming is the best time to go into depth over whatever issue comes up right then; this often leads to a fight or a reactionary response that may not be appropriate or helpful. It would be much better to talk in depth about a subject when everybody is ready and calm, knowing the discussion will come up. Then both people have had time to think about it and can talk *unemotionally* about whatever the issue is. Being reactive versus proactive causes stress and tension where there doesn't need to be any. Weekly staff meetings are an active way couples can avoid a lot of anger, apologies, hurt feelings, financial mistakes, and needless worry.

2. *Preserves romance and connection.*

A weekly staff meeting also allows a date not to become a staff meeting. Why ruin a wonderful night out by discussing things like finances and issues with the kids? With a staff meeting already in place, you know you can talk about it later. When there is no planned time to actually talk, it is very easy for couples to slide into staff meeting items while they are out on a date. The weekly staff meeting allows you to talk about the kids or finances at an appropriate time and leaves date nights to delve into other interesting things you both want to explore.

3. *Moves a couple out of constant-crisis mode.*

It is so important to go through a list of the normal, repeating issues in your life as a married couple and talk about how you are going to handle these areas. I have seen couple after couple argue over how he is always gone at night or how she loves church more than being with him. I have watched couples argue over poker night or his spontaneous invitation for friends to come over after work with no notice or regard for his wife. I have watched couples have the same argument about how much was spent on groceries week after week with no solution. Couples fight over a whole host of things, but having a staff meeting every week can help resolve these repeating offenses.

New solutions to these types of issues—over schedules, spending, or friends—can be hashed out in an unemotional, systematic way. These answers won't come in the spur of the moment when one or both people are mad. The staff meeting allows both parties to make their case calmly and thoroughly. How many of us have thought of all kinds of things we should have said after an argument instead of during one? A pre-determined staff meeting means we have time to think about our point of view and the reasons we want to do something before we discuss anything with our spouse. Also, it allows one or both of the partners to table (talk about it later) a topic that is maybe getting too heated in that meeting so they can become calm or gain more information about it.

Sometimes hard things need to be discussed. It's tough to have these kinds of discussions, but it's better to have a preset time to talk about things than just reacting in the heat of the moment to a complaint and then being mad at each other. This is almost always counterproductive. Think about it—would a good company not have a staff meeting because a couple of the employees were upset with one another? No. They would still have the staff meeting where the disagreement or crisis would make the agenda.

HOLDING A STAFF MEETING

Couples in great marriages have staff meetings so that man and wife can be on the same page and talk things through. Couples in bad marriages stay angry and punish each other, refusing to get over their selfishness without pressing forward to something good and helpful. Let me give you some ideas about how they can work.

In terms of timing, you and your spouse should hold a staff meeting every week for one to three hours. As far as when to have a staff meeting, it is up to what works best for both of you. They should last long enough to take care of business, which some weeks means only an hour, while others may require several hours. You can always table non-urgent topics for the following week. It is not always easy to find a regular time, but usually, there is some time on the weekend that can be repurposed for a staff meeting.

My wife and I would sit down on Saturday afternoons starting at one o'clock to discuss the coming week and the various issues we know about. Recently we have found that Sunday at 4 p.m. is a better time for our current life stage with the kids out of the house. We find it very helpful to prepare some sort of simple agenda. (I have given you a sample agenda in this chapter.)

Sometimes your spouse or your schedule don't cooperate to have one big staff meeting. I don't think this is ideal but you can have a staff meeting over several days with each topic being a different day.

One of the things that stifles a good staff meeting and a ridiculously great marriage is to have the belief that one person's initial statements on an issue settles the discussion. This is never true. People can change their mind with new information. There must be the idea that at first everybody is putting in their impressions, ideas, and limited perspective. It is only after a more thorough discussion, research, and prayer that a final decision can be made.

Do a favor for your marriage and life by inserting a staff meeting into your week. If something is a reoccurring issue, then throw out perspectives and solutions and seek new ideas from your spouse. You will build a great life together this way. Neither one of you needs to be the one with the answer for everything. It is amazing how helpful a regular discussion of the issues can be. It allows you to accomplish what needs to be done for a healthy relationship: play when it is time to play, work when it is time to work, and figure out new ideas when those are needed. I have provided a sample agenda below with various topics and questions to guide you. There may be other questions that need to be added and tailored to your circumstances. Do whatever works the best for you.

Sample Agenda

The bolded topics are what I would suggest for a normal agenda. I have offered some questions and suggestions to explore this topic. You don't have to use my questions or comments, but if they are helpful, then use them.

Schedule—work, dates, friends, fun, vacations, church, workouts

What is your schedule this next week?

What is my schedule this next week?

Finances—income, expenses, management, giving, saving

Go over where the family is meeting or not meeting the budget.

Talk about what can and cannot be purchased this next week.

What monies need to be spent this week?

Can we purchase this or do we need to wait?

Are we still on track for the holiday or party or vacation?

Have we spent too much on anything so far this month?

(Note: This is not a full-on budget meeting, just an update. See the chapter on habit #13 for more about this.)

Kids—relationship, respect, routines, responsibility, rules, resources (the 6 R's)

When you have children still living at home, this section of the staff meeting may take up the most time. Go through the six R's below. Discuss each child and where progress needs to be made in each area. This allows you both to work together to develop an enjoyable family by tackling problematic areas and developing a plan for each child. We can also use this opportunity to examine ourselves when it comes to our interactions with our children and the example we set for them. It really can be wonderful to raise a family when you have a plan and work together. (For more on this, visit www.ptlb.com/audio-downloads and download the *Four Keys to Be a Great Family* podcast.)

Relationship:

How is Dad's relationships with child 1, child 2, and so on? Mom?

Which child needs more time, love, or attention?

What other relationships are becoming important to the children?

Are there any relationships you are concerned about?

How do we deal with a relationship that is becoming damaging?

How do we encourage more beneficial relationships for the kids?

Respect:

Do our children receive value, praise, and encouragement every day?

What are ways we can increase the amount of respect going to the kids?

Are they respectful of us and each other?

How do you want to teach respect for adults?

How do you want to teach the kids to say NO at the appropriate times and in the appropriate ways?

Routines:

Which routines do they need to know about for their next phase of development? *(For example, bedtime, homework, wake-up, morning, lunch, arrive home, dinner, after dinner, evening, family devotions, driving, filling the car with gas, sports, church, out with friends, parties.)*

Which routines are not working?

Which routines should we emphasize or practice this week?

Responsibility:

Where are our children making unwise or bad choices?

Which areas of irresponsibility are we going to focus on this week?

Are we going to use words or actions to teach our children to make a better choice the next time? What particular subset of one of these?

How are we going to encourage or influence better choices?

How are we going to remind ourselves not to get angry as they learn?

What will we not focus on this week?

Rules:

Do our children understand our rules, traditions, and boundaries?

How are we going to explain our traditions?

What traditions do we need to invent for our family this month?

What rules will keep us from having a fight with our kids in a few years?

Resources:

What resources do each of our children need this week? *(For example, financial, intellectual, role models, emotional, relational, physical, skill development, knowledge of the hidden rules.)*

How will we introduce these resources to our kids?

How will we monitor these resources in their life?

Concerned about…?

Both parties should be able to bring up things they are concerned about. A staff meeting is an opportunity to talk about things before they become a real problem.

"I think we are going to need to decide about the summer vacation within the next two months."

"I don't think we can put off fixing the car much longer—what are your thoughts about the repair?"

Remember, the goal of a staff meeting is to get organized and on the same page about things—not to hammer your point of view. There is a way to find wisdom. Some typical issues that cause concern for many couples and can be added to the agenda deal with:

- Home
- Work
- Relatives
- Future plans
- Vacation, getting away

Spouses in great marriages can discuss almost anything without getting angry, or demanding that only one opinion is possible, namely their own. Stay calm if the other person brings up something you are not ready to come to a resolution about. Realize every person sees various things from different points of view. Work with your spouse instead of against them. There is a way for you and your spouse to be on the same side. You don't have to leave each staff meeting having resolved every issue. In fact, you won't, but the discussion will spur new ideas, new potential solutions, and new levels of cooperation.

Expectations

Another agenda item can be around setting expectations for next week or future plans. Inevitably, the husband or the wife will expect something to happen in the next week that is not necessarily top of the mind for the other one. This is not a reason to get upset just because they were not thinking like you. Bring up what is important to you during the next week, so it is not a surprise to the other one. If one person has a big thing at work, they should mention it. If one person is excited about an activity or a friend, they should make sure to talk about it. If there is a big bill due or a crucial anniversary coming, one of you needs to bring it up. If you are expecting your spouse to do a particular thing, mention it. If your children are having a big play or game and both parents should be there, discuss it. Don't expect the other person to be a mind reader—they aren't! Communicate the expectations so neither of you fails. The goal is to have a win-win for everyone, not to fail. This is the kind of language you can use to communicate expectations:

We have an obligation later today. I am expecting you to (do something) this morning, this afternoon, this evening.

I'm expecting to get to (do something) this weekend, this Friday, this day.

I am hoping to be able to (do something) this month, or within 6 months, within a year, and so forth.

Remember that (child 1) has a project due on Friday and he will need your help with it.

We have dinner at the Jones' house at 6:00 on Friday night. Can you be home by 5:30 so we can be there on time?

Our anniversary is next month. How do you want to celebrate it this year?

If you discover you have different expectations about a particular time or event, then have a calm discussion about it. There are always ways it can work out. "I'm sorry, but I was expecting you to be home for dinner at six, not eight! Is there a way you can be home in time for dinner tomorrow night?" There are always options that have not been considered yet but will allow for the most benefit to the most people. To have a great marriage, you have to think options and possibilities instead of "I want what I want." Stay flexible and realize that your idea of what is perfect is not necessarily perfect for the other person or the whole family. Having these discussions before the event happens allows for new plans and peace. Waiting until expectations become reality often causes fights, disappointment, and hurt feelings.

Let me give you an illustration. There was a time when I had an idyllic view of our whole family doing various trips together. Even as the kids got older, I was forcing everyone to go on every outing. It was just not possible to have everybody go on every outing every time without major disruptions. So my wife and I had a most profitable discussion about my expectations, and over a period of weeks, I realized I needed to be much more flexible.

Great marriages don't just happen—they are planned, prayed about, and purposefully formed. It seems many people have the idea that if two people are "right" for one another, then it will be easy to have a great marriage. This is not true. Even if you are naturally compatible, making a marriage work requires both spouses to work through the various things that come up in a marriage. Use the discussion points I provided as a guide to get you started and grow from there. I know of no successful business that succeeds without planning and communication. The greatest team and business you will ever be a part of is your marriage; therefore, to maximize your marriage in every direction, plan for the staff meeting every week.

Substitute Kindness for Sarcasm

George was a sarcastic and gifted put-down artist. He was the life of parties with his speeches and observations of normal, everyday folks. He could have pursued a career in stand-up comedy. He worked a normal job and wanted a ridiculously good marriage, but he was not going to get one unless he changed some things. It was a difficult pill for George to swallow that he would have to talk to his girlfriend differently than how he wanted to talk to her. He wanted to play to the audience in his head when he noticed her weaknesses, failings, and areas where she struggled. It took a lot of time and a number of girlfriends before he could control his tongue enough to keep a relationship going. Eventually, he did learn how to talk to his girlfriend lovingly so as not to offend her. This one habit changed George's life. He went from lonely, arrogant, and cruel, to loving, encouraging, and kind just by controlling his tongue.

How we speak to another human being is crucial. It will make or break a relationship. One of the counter-intuitive habits of this culture is to eliminate sarcasm and replace it with kindness.

THE DAMAGE OF SARCASM

There are two crucial rules to have a relationship with someone. The first is *don't offend or abuse the people you want to be friends with*. Isn't this an obvious rule? And yet this is what sarcasm is—offensiveness and abuse masquerading as clever rudeness and witty criticism. We need to be kind and loving to the people we want a lasting relationship with, right? Yet, our culture implies we can have a relationship built on put-downs, sarcasm, and making our friends the butt of the joke. I think you will find the sarcasm habit that makes you a hit in big groups will actually harm your personal relationships.

If you think it is working for you, then you are most likely the one telling the jokes, not receiving them. You are the one with the power, not the person dealing with the verbal abuse coming from his "friend." Relationships work so much better when people are nice to one another. The Golden Rule, "Treat others as you want to be treated," really does work.

The second rule of relationships is *relationships have to be guarded and protected*. A ridiculously great marriage doesn't just happen. One or both spouses have to want the relationship more than the thousand other things they could have or do. And the relationship needs to be guarded and protected against all sorts of outside forces and damage. If I had a prized '57 Chevy, I would not purposely cut scratches into the paint job. I would protect it and guard against others damaging it too. Being sarcastic is like scratching the paint job on a pristine car and then wondering why it doesn't look as good anymore. I find way too many couples (men, especially, but an increasing number of women) who think someone is keeping track of when they said something funny. Like they get points for being sarcastically funny at their spouse's expense. That is not the way a healthy relationship works. You get marriage points for how good you make your spouse feel, not for how much your friends will laugh when they hear what you said.

Unfortunately, many shows portray the family as one that is openly rude, cutting, sarcastic, and even mean to their family members. These TV shows and movies don't mean to be modeling behavior for people; they just want to be funny and make a profit. But in truth, they are destructive. People are seeing the picture of this type of family and imitating the behavior. It is absolutely cancerous to relationships.

This destructive habit of sarcasm and put-downs draws laughs and has become the norm for real life. But your life is not a comedy sketch. It is not a TV show with laugh tracks and paid actors. Your life is made up of real people you care about and who care about you, so hurting them is senseless. The habit of sarcasm is one of the most destructive patterns I see present in hurting marriages. It is considered clever and fun to be sarcastic to people, but it is the height of rudeness and destroys the relationship. One of the first things I tell couples to do is to stop being sarcastic. It never helps but always hurts. It is one person gaining at the expense of the other, the very opposite of what is needed for a ridiculously great marriage.

Now does sarcasm have a place where it can be used? Yes, I believe so. I have discovered when a person speaks in public, they can use sarcasm as a way to gain attention. It is especially helpful when the speaker is the butt of the joke. This is the essence of most comedians' stand-up routines. People enjoy laughing at others' mistakes and can learn from the faux pas of others. But understand that the speaker cannot make their kids or their spouse or their friends the focus of their wit and put-downs if they want to have any friends when they come off the stage. The best stand-up comedians are incredibly gentle and kind off the platform and usually use pretend characters, themselves, or non-existent friends and relatives as the point of the joke. Understand that the television sitcom is not real and the put-downs on the show are about non-real characters, so the actors who are playing those characters are not offended by the sarcasm because it is the role and not the real person.

Another hurtful way people use sarcasm is as a way of saying something to their spouse or their children they don't dare say straight up. The person using sarcasm is hoping the other person will get the message and make the desired change. This style of communication doesn't cause change; it causes resentment. If you want change, then have an open, honest discussion about what you do want and what is hurting, wounding, or troubling you. In my life, there are three rules I get from Ephesians 4:29, which says,

> *Let no unwholesome word proceed from your mouth, but only such a word as is good for edification according to the need of the moment, so that it will give grace to those who hear.*

- Is what I am about to say positive?
- Is what I am about to say going to build up or help the other person?
- Does what I am about to say really need to be said?

Good relationships are built on real conversations, not hidden codes and half-truths. It is better to be direct but kind.

LEARNING TO ELIMINATE SARCASM

One of the most difficult elements about sarcasm is what it often turns into— caustic contempt. The Gottman Institute, who many experts consider to be the premier marriage research group in America, has found contempt to be the number one factor that tears couples apart. When contempt enters the marriage, it is like acid poured on the bonds of affection and connection. People who are focused on criticizing their partners miss a whopping fifty percent of positive things their partners are doing, and they see negativity where there is none. People who give their partner the cold shoulder—by deliberately ignoring the partner or responding minimally—damage the relationship significantly. They make their partner feel worthless and invisible, like they're not there, not valued. Treating your partner with contempt and criticism kills love. It is the death knell of relationships.

Learning to eliminate sarcasm is a hard habit to break but essential to do so. If you like to use sarcasm, you might be thinking, "What am I going to talk about if I don't use sarcasm?" This was a real question that popped into my mind when my mentor confronted me about giving up sarcasm many years ago. He knew my level of sarcasm had to go in order to build lasting relationships. My sarcasm was too caustic and was getting in the way. I thought my relationship issues had to do with everybody else's problem and not mine. Truly, once I eliminated sarcasm and negativity from my speech patterns, I didn't have a lot to say to the young ladies I dated, so I had to learn to do something else—to listen and ask questions instead. This turned out to be a very good thing for me, because rather than monologue or say the put-downs or sarcastic comebacks that immediately came to my mind, I would ask them to explain more of what they were talking about. In the beginning, this was my only defense against my own destructive tendency to be sarcastic, rude, and negative. Now I live by four rules to stay away from sarcasm:

Say it boring.

Say it lovingly.

Say it positively.

Say it straight.

I can remember in high school having a relationship with a young lady where the total sum of our relationship was insulting one another for two hours. It's no wonder the relationship didn't last. It was built entirely on physical attractiveness and verbal abuse masquerading as a witty conversation. I thought I was so clever and good at the put-down. Unfortunately, I was too good, which was one of the major things I needed to unlearn as I grew up and began to follow a Christian way of life.

Recently, I was preparing a talk for a group of about a hundred couples who were coming to one of my workshops. We had been meeting for a few weeks and the couples were growing significantly. I had hoped to cover two more topics that are crucial to marriages. I began to pray about which one of the two topics to cover in the next talk, and as I was praying, I saw a clear sign scrolling across my mind that said KINDNESS—in big, block capital letters. I remember arguing with the Lord, "Kindness is not that strong of a topic, is it Lord?" Back and forth I went in prayer pushing my two topics, but God kept pushing this "weak" idea of kindness. Finally, I said, "Okay, I will do some more research on kindness, but the research I have done in the past has not unearthed much." Well, the research on kindness I found was shocking. It turns out that kindness is now recognized as the primary trait that predicts marital stability and marital health.[1] Kindness makes each partner feel cared for, understood, and validated—it makes us feel loved.

There's a great deal of evidence showing the more someone receives kindness, or even witnesses kindness, the more they will be kind themselves. Kindness leads to upward spirals of love and generosity in a relationship and among people. There are many reasons why relationships fail, but if you look at what drives the deterioration of many relationships, it is often a breakdown of kindness. As the normal stresses of a life pile up—with children, careers, friends, in-laws, and other distractions that crowd out time for romance and intimacy—couples often put less effort into their relationship and let the petty grievances tear them apart. In most marriages, levels of satisfaction drop dramatically within the first few years together. But among couples who live happily together for years, the spirit of kindness and generosity guides them forward.

You can learn to substitute kindness for sarcasm. There are four ways to communicate kindness to your spouse.

1. *Speak kindly and make thoughtful requests.*

The Scriptures are clear:

> *Death and life are in the power of the tongue, and those*
> *who love it will eat its fruit. (Proverbs 18:21 NASB)*

> *Do not let kindness and truth leave you; bind them around your*
> *neck, write them on the tablet of your heart. (Proverbs 3:3)*

Oftentimes we are too strong on truth and not generous enough with kindness, and we end up eroding our relationships. We should be thinking, "What kind thing can I say to my spouse?" According to author Lawrence Lovasik, "Kind words are a creative force, a power that concurs in the building up of all that is good, and energy that showers blessings upon the world."[2] For a ridiculously great marriage, we must build in more kindness.

2. *Focus on the positives in your spouse.*

In every relationship, you get what you look for. If you focus on what is wrong with the other person, you will get more of it. If, however, you focus on what is good, right, true, and praiseworthy in the other person, you will get more of that (Phil. 4:7, 8). Sarcasm needs to be eliminated because it finds and exploits weaknesses. It doesn't build up but wounds. It is good for jokes but not relationships.

Dr. John Gottman explained in an interview that those who are great at relationships are always scanning their partner for things they can appreciate and praise. The opposite is also true. Those people who have bad relationships are always pointing out where their spouse messed up or isn't measuring up to what is desired.[3] This is what sarcasm does; it puts the focus on the negative, the weakness, the mistake, the oddity. Ruthlessly substitute kindness for sarcasm (men, I am talking to you.)

3. *Speak kindly during fights or disagreements.*

The hardest time to practice kindness is during a fight. Those who have a great marriage do not let their disagreements become wounding. A disagreement should be a difference of perspective that is solvable because both parties stay flexible. The thinking should be, "Since the relationship is more important than some difference in perspective, let's talk about this and grow together." Letting contempt and aggression spiral out of control during a conflict can inflict irrevocable damage on a relationship. Dr. Julie Gottman explains, "Kindness doesn't mean that we don't express our anger, but kindness informs how we choose to express the anger. You can throw spears at your partner. Or you can explain why you're hurt and angry, and that's the kinder path."[4]

People who are bad at relationships attack, blame, shame, and heap guilt upon others. The people who maintain strong relationships don't do that; they wrap their ideas and changes in kindness so that a dialogue can follow. It is important to remember that even when people are frustrated in a relationship, there are lots of positive things going on. Dr. John Gottman explains the difference between "disasters" and "masters" in marriage. Disasters will say, "You're late." "What's wrong with you?" "You're just like your mom." Masters will say, "I feel bad for picking on you about your lateness, and I know it's not your fault, but it's really annoying that you're late again."[5] We can all become masters by learning to speak kindly, even in fights and disagreements.

4. *Celebrate your spouse's good news.*

One of the greatest predictors of marital longevity is whether each spouse celebrates the successes of their partner. If it must always be about you, your marriage is in trouble. This is an overlooked area but will pay rich dividends for your relationship. The Bible says in 1 Corinthians 13 that love is kind and rejoices in the truth. You can speak volumes of kindness by making a big deal about your spouse's accomplishments. When your spouse tells you about some victory but is greeted by a "that's nice, honey" response, this indicates disaster for the relationship.[6]

It is exceptionally kind for a person to make a big deal about another person's good things. When my wife finished her doctorate degree in nursing, I made sure we spent considerable time after her graduation to delve deep into this achievement. I asked her who would be the most meaningful to tell? Who did she think would be the most shocked by her achieving this milestone? What did she want to do to celebrate? How did she think this was going to change her career? I invented every question I could think of to help her explore her feelings and thoughts. It was a delightful time of joy, reactions, ideas, goals, and excitement I had never seen in her.

Don't miss these injections of love, even if the celebration or accomplishment is minor. Did your spouse get a promotion, some recognition, finish a project, achieve a goal, win an award, or make a new friend? All of these and a hundred other things need to be celebrated. Too often we are so self-focused on our own accomplishments to get excited about others' successes. But everyone needs a cheerleader from time to time. One of the greatest ways to speak volumes of love to your spouse is to be a cheerleader for their triumphs. One 2006 study proved couples who celebrated their victories and triumphs went on to stability and marital health. The couples who divorced could not celebrate the wins of their spouse. They were too self-focused and their relationship fell apart.[7]

My line of work allows me to listen to a lot of couples talk to one another. If I hear them putting each other down, I know it is not a healthy relationship. Develop the habit of saying positive things to your spouse. Sarcastic comments work on TV for laughs but destroy actual relationships. There is no laugh track in your home. No one applauds when you unleash a zinger against your spouse. These behaviors destroy your relationship.

EDIFY AND BUILD UP YOUR SPOUSE

Every time you speak to your spouse, you have the chance to build them up, encourage them, and develop a greater bond. Think of healthy conversation like how athletes view their own performance. Those athletes who realize that every pitch in baseball should be a great pitch; every trip down the basketball floor should be a great shot; every shot in golf should have focus and a purpose—these are the winning athletes. Likewise, every time you talk with your spouse should build your relationship. Don't just throw-up verbally on your spouse and expect things to be ok. And never try to get a laugh at their expense. Take advantage of the wonder of talking to them using kindness and love to build up a ridiculously great relationship.

Here's another way to view it. What if you had a friend named Bob, who every time you saw him, he always threw a glass of cold water in your face…every time. It wouldn't take more than three times before you would start avoiding Bob. You would start looking for ways to minimize time with him. Throwing cold water in someone's face is what sarcasm is emotionally. It backs a person up. It is offensive—the very opposite of kindness and love.

Again,

Say it boring.

Say it straight.

Say it positive.

Say it lovingly.

See if you can be clever enough to have a normal conversation with your spouse without sarcasm. Focus specifically on kindness. I am amazed at the number of people who cannot do it. Understand how truly destructive sarcasm is. Marriages significantly improve when sarcasm is banned as a form of communication. Communicate kindness to your spouse instead.

Speak kindly and make thoughtful requests.

Focus on the positives in the person.

Speak kindly even during fights or disagreements.

Celebrate their good news and accomplishments.

Just as George the put-down artist found lasting love by abandoning sarcasm, you too can embrace love and connection by making a habit of talking about a person's strengths and not their weaknesses. How can you speak words of kindness to your spouse? Find a way to frame your discussion as a positive, even if you may want to say something sarcastic or downright mean. Find out what they are excited about or interested in and talk with them about those things. Try it!

Apologize When You've Blown It

You may have heard the romantic tag line, "Love means never having to say you're sorry." While this sounds nice, it is entirely false. Real love means always being ready to say you're sorry. But how? Isn't it easier to just ignore the issue and pretend it never happened? Isn't it easier to hope your spouse will just "get over it"? Sadly, some people choose these methods as their go-to solutions for when they've blown it and then wonder why their relationship isn't so great. But couples with ridiculously great marriages know when and how to apologize. The apology is one of the habits we must develop to have great relationships.

Apologies can be simple or complex. They can be over in a few seconds or take years to work out fully. It's a given you will offend your spouse. You will say something mean or do something without understanding the ramifications. This means that if you want a good marriage, each spouse will need to get used to saying, "I'm sorry," "I apologize," "I shouldn't have done that," or "Please forgive me." If you or your spouse have never apologized, you are not dealing with reality. Say: "I was wrong," "I am so sorry," "That was stupid of me," "Would you forgive me for my attitude?" Apologies are always helpful. This is true even when you haven't necessarily done anything wrong.

Realize there are really three "people" in your marriage: you, your spouse, and your marriage. You may not have been wrong in what you said, but saying it damaged the relationship, therefore an apology is needed. There will be times when you need to apologize for things you didn't do that would have made the relationship better. There will be times you will need to apologize for things you said that hurt your spouse deeply even though that was not your intention. There will be times when you will need to apologize for not understanding or being sensitive to what is going on behind the scenes.

Let me give you an example. On me and my wife's anniversary, I had to apologize for something I didn't know I'd done. Why did I have to? Because not doing so would have ruined our whole night!

My wife was trying to get home so we could leave for our anniversary dinner. She had texted me earlier to let me know she would be home at 6:15. So because I had a few extra minutes, I went out to get a card, a balloon, flowers, and candy for her. I went to three different stores to get just the right items—I wanted to get it right. At about 5:45, Dana called me very upset that I was not home and ready to go to dinner. I was confused and shocked, and I quickly explained that I had no idea she had gotten home so quickly. She had sent *two* text messages to tell me she was able to get away earlier, which I had not received.

I dashed home as fast as I could, apologizing for not being there. Just as I was apologizing, her texts vibrated into my phone. It helped that I could show her I got them at 5:50, but what really helped was that I came in with an apologizing spirit. It was clear to my wife that I wanted to be with her just as much as she wanted to be with me, so we went on with the evening and had a terrific time. It would not have helped if I had come in with an arrogant spirit proving I hadn't messed up, and she had no reason to be upset with me. I was more interested in the marriage than being right.

I have met with hundreds of couples who never admit they do anything wrong in the marriage. They just expect their spouse to suck up the hurt, pain, and disrespect. What's sad is these couples always become cold toward one another. It is time to admit we are not perfect. Our spouse knows we mess up.

Apologies allow us to build a strong relationship in the presence of those imperfections. Without them, there is no clearing away of hurts that occur in every relationship. What if we never cleaned up our dishes after lunch or dinner? There would be piles of uneaten food and bugs crawling all over our kitchens. This is what a marriage without apologies is like. Admitting wrongdoings can work wonders to build trust and repair damage between you.

THREE TYPES OF APOLOGIES

I was taught a short and a long process for effective apologies, but I believe there are actually three types of apologies. We should be comfortable making any of these three to move the relationship forward—the quick apology, the specific apology, and the long apology.

1. *The quick apology.*

This type of apology comes with the desire to have the relationship mended quickly. It is not a formal apology but rather a humbling of oneself, saying the words in a soft and gentle tone (as in the case of my anniversary story above). "I am so sorry." "I apologize for how this came off." "I wish I had received your texts, and I am sorry this evening is not getting off to the start we had both wanted."

A quick apology is ideal for a misunderstanding where a humble attitude can prevent it from turning into a fight. It is often a plea for understanding. Sometimes a quick apology is not accepted because the other person believes this issue is a bigger deal than a quick "I am so sorry" can fix. I often suggest that couples start with a quick apology and then keep talking to see if there is more that is needed.

This quick apology is often two steps of the long apology: a humble and gentle "I-am-so-sorry" attitude and an admission of wrongdoing. The relationship is healed when one spouse acknowledges they hurt the other person. The other day, I became irritated because people were pushing ahead of my family in line. I allowed my irritation with the other people to cause me to speak curtly and angrily to my wife. I needed to apologize for being irritated and angry toward her. She thanked me for acknowledging that I was out of line, and it was over and done in thirty seconds. We went on to have a wonderful time because I had admitted my attitude and anger was inappropriate.

In my marriage seminars, I give actual phrases to say for quick apologies, because many people aren't skilled at giving apologies to others. Say these phrases multiple times to your spouse as practice so that you can say them about real stuff in your marriage.

"I am sorry for _____. Would you please forgive me?"

"I need to apologize for the way I acted earlier; you didn't deserve that."

"I realize that I hurt you with what I did and said. It was wrong."

"Would you please forgive me and let me help repair our relationship?"

"I don't want to hurt you, but I can tell I've done something wrong. Would you help me understand how I have hurt you so I can do better?"

These short apologies let your spouse know you are aware there is a problem and you care enough to do something about it. Much of the time this will be all that is needed to clear the air. Don't be upset if your spouse thinks more is needed than a quick apology for some offenses. That's when this next type of apology comes in to play.

2. *The specific apology.*

Sometimes, you need this second kind of apology for when you did something that was not overwhelmingly bad but your spouse needs you to know what you did. This apology starts with a gentle spirit, then specifies what you did or didn't do. Practice these phrases until it is easy for you to apologize about specific things you did or did not do.

> *"I am sorry for stepping on your dress."*

> *"I apologize for accusing you when I didn't have all the facts."*

> *"I am really sorry that we got our wires crossed and I forgot to put the trash out."*

> *"I apologize for my stupidity ... for my laziness ... for what I said at the party..."*

> *"I apologize for jumping to negative conclusions about what was going on..."*

You get the idea. The specific apology is about naming a specific wrong. If you did something to offend your spouse, apologize for that specific offense. Don't beat around the bush; just say you were wrong for doing or not doing what you did or didn't do. You don't lose points for admitting you were wrong—you gain them. This lets your spouse know that you really do understand what you did. If your spouse can receive your apology, realize you really meant it, and did not intend to hurt them, this is a repair of the relationship.

3. *The long apology.*

It is crucial for everyone in a marriage to know how to repair the relationship through this deeper type of apology. You will need this long apology at some point in your marriage if not regularly. I would put this list on your phone or bathroom mirror or refrigerator as a ready-to-access guide through these steps. Here are the six steps of a long apology.

1. Gentle and humble in spirit and demeanor.

2. Seek education—What did I do wrong?

3. Admit you were wrong.

4. Ask for forgiveness.

5. Discuss a repentance plan.

6. Test for openness.

This third type of apology is absolutely crucial in helping marriages stay healthy. It is instrumental in moving a marriage toward healing after the stupidity and selfishness that inevitably happens. Just know when you begin this process, there probably will be huge tension in the relationship. There will be difficulty carrying on conversation, so we often want to rush through this, but don't. This repair process takes time, usually forty-five to ninety minutes, but it is totally worth it. You will either give this process the time it needs, or you will have three days to three weeks of uncomfortable tension with the issue always looming in the background. Heal the relationship and clear the air.

Realize, it is your spouse who gets to say if the offense was serious or a simple error. All of us tend to minimize our own mistakes while magnifying the offenses and insults of others. When an offense is repeated often enough or is deeply wounding, then it becomes a serious offense. How do you know your spouse is hurt beyond what is necessary for a quick or specific apology? Ask them.

Another signal is when the other person is stand-offish and moves away from you emotionally, mentally, or physically. You may not even know what you did, but you'll find out if you want to heal your marriage.

I have instructed many couples to memorize the six steps. I want them committed to memory. Take the time to learn how to use this long apology process so it becomes a part of your relational toolkit. You'll need it.

Step One: Gentle and humble in spirit and demeanor. (Prov. 15:1)

To apologize in a genuine manner, gentleness is necessary. Proverbs 15:1 says, "A gentle answer turns away wrath, but a harsh word stirs up anger." I have found many men have to almost whisper to be gentle enough to allow their wives to engage. Too much emotion or drama, and she will be flooded and likely shut down. Be prepared to stay gentle and calm during the other person's description of your offense.

The conversation can begin by saying something like, "I sense I have hurt you. I can guess I said something or did something that wounded you. It was not my intention to hurt you, so I would like to understand what I did, so I don't do it again. Would you share with me how I hurt you so I can change? I want our relationship to be whole again."

Step Two: Seek education. (Luke 17:3)

Most of the time, we don't know how or when we have hurt our spouse. We are just moving through life doing our thing, focused on what we want. Many men and women are dumbfounded when their spouse begins to open up about how and when they were hurt. The offender is stunned about the damage the offense caused. It is so helpful if the offender says, "Would you educate me about how this hurt you?" That's when the floodgates open. This question is an invitation to the wounded one. It fills them with the hope that things may change and they will not be hurt anymore. It suggests there is real caring and they will be treated with dignity.

It is true we often don't understand how our words, actions, attitudes, and omissions really damage the other person. So this step is about taking the time to ask your spouse how you have hurt them. You do this because you want to understand what you did so you won't hurt them like that again. You are seeking education about what you did that caused the hurt. Luke 17:3 says, "Be on guard. If your brother sins, rebuke him (educate him); and if he repents, forgive him" (emphasis mine). A rebuke is painful for you to hear but essential if the other person is to forgive you later. You must understand your offense from their point of view.

Listen intently and repeat what your spouse said to make sure you heard it correctly. Do not move through this step too fast. This is the part of the apology that can take forty-five minutes to an hour; it is the real magic of the apology. It is where they are getting the hurt off their chest. Don't defend yourself or tell them they don't understand what happened properly. Just listen and let them share the incident from their perspective. This is not about your defense. This is about their need to share with you how they experienced what happened, which is the real issue. If they misheard or didn't see it accurately, there will be time later to clear it up, but now is the time to just listen. Make sure you are really paying attention, listening for their emotional reaction to what happened. Try to understand what they experienced so your apology will work effectively.

During this education part, you will want to explain; you will want to tell them things they don't know; you will want to change the subject because this is really uncomfortable, *but don't do it!* Don't stop this process; let them get everything out. Let them talk. You will be able to get to your defense later if it is needed. They saw the offense from a completely different perspective than you did. You need to see it from their point of view. If you can abandon your point of view for the moment, this will help with the next part of the apology process.

Step Three: Admit you were wrong. (1 John 1:9)

One of the most important things to say in an apology is "I was wrong." "I shouldn't have treated you that way; that was wrong." Good relationships need both people to admit they have been wrong at times. Practice saying you were wrong. Don't cop out and say you may have been mistaken. Say the words, "I was wrong." It is a big step, but it will do a lot of wonderful things in a relationship when both parties can admit they have been wrong. Let me give you a few examples.

I was wrong when I pushed you to try that new activity.

I was wrong when I embarrassed you in front of your friends.

I was wrong when I got angry at you even though I wasn't even mad at you at all.

I was wrong when I reacted to what you were saying without listening all the way through to what you were talking about.

I was wrong when I walked away without letting you speak.

I was wrong when I told the kids you were wrong about what you wanted them to do.

I was wrong when I signed you up to help with the school outing without asking you.

I was wrong to spend the money without checking with you.

I was wrong when I Facebooked with my old flame from high school.

I was wrong when I spent a bunch of money on clothes without talking with you first.

I was wrong to look at the pornography.

I was wrong to steal the money from the company.

I was wrong not to call you when I was going to be late.

I was wrong to spend more time with my friends this weekend than with you.

See all the things we can be wrong about? I'm sure you can add more to this list! Let your spouse know you are so sorry they were hurt. Apologizing that you hurt them and acknowledging the damage it caused to your relationship is a big deal. Use the word "wrong." Let it settle in. They need to hear you say it.

Usually, it is best to not mount a defense for your actions until after you have admitted you were wrong for some aspect of the situation. Your spouse needs to see you coming to repair the relationship rather than defending yourself. If you jump too quickly to your excuses, then they know you really don't care about them. If your reasons for what happened are valid, but you wait to bring them up until after your spouse feels heard, then they will be able to listen to your "reasons."

Every once in a while, a wound, hurt, or offense is a result of a complete misunderstanding. Sometimes it really is just a total misunderstanding. If the other person has been heard and understood, then you can share the misunderstanding with them. Be warned—if you are always claiming your offenses are "misunderstandings," your spouse will realize you are unwilling to accept responsibility and the relationship will slip a few steps backward.

Step Four: Ask for forgiveness. (Matt. 6:15)

John finally heard what Vanessa was saying. He was stunned by how he had hurt her. He was insensitive, self-focused, and disrespectful. He had been living his life as he saw fit, never imagining that he was constantly wounding her through his selfishness. He actually thought she was enjoying the life they had built just as much as he was. It never occurred to him that he was living in a one-sided relationship where he got all the benefits and she got all the work and disrespect.

When she explained this to him, his whole body was limp. Because of his body language, Vanessa saw he really got it. She had been shoved down to fifth place on his priority structure. The air in the room was heavy with depression and discouragement. John finally had the energy to say to Vanessa, "I was wrong. Will you forgive me?" She could feel it was real and believed there was a great possibility change might come. It didn't feel hollow. Thankfully, this marked a turning point in their marriage.

After admitting you are wrong, ask if they can forgive you for the offense or hurt. It is very helpful to ask if the person forgives you because this gauges where they are in the apology process. If they say, "Yes, I forgive you," then things can get back to normal—you have won a renewed relationship. But if they say *no*, you have some work to do. Ask *why*. Usually this is because they don't believe you really understand how much that offense hurt them.

Hopefully, they will tell you a little more about it. You'll need to apologize and ask for forgiveness again. Realize they may say no for a number of reasons:

- It may be that they don't think you are calm enough to really understand what you did (go back to being gentler).

- It could be they don't think you really want to know what hurts them (go back to ask them to educate you).

- It could be they don't believe you really understand you are wrong (go back to your admission of wrongdoing).

- It could be they don't think you are ready to be forgiven (maybe they need to think about what it means to let go of this offense against you).

- It could be because it's a repeated offense and they think you will do it again.

If this last one is the case, you need to move on to the next step—form a repentance plan. This is the way for you to prove you're ready and serious about making amends.

Step Five: Form a repentance plan. (Luke 3:8)

If the offense is a repeated offense or very serious, you and your spouse will have to decide what to do so you won't ever do it again. My recommendation is to set up a repentance plan with your spouse. If we really feel bad about what we have done and have truly changed our mind about an offense, then we need to be willing to make changes. It's up to you to determine how valuable the relationship is to you—if it's important, you will work to change.

I recently heard of a woman who discovered an explicit series of sexting messages on her husband's phone with another woman in another city. She confronted him, "What is this?" Her first reaction was "I want a divorce," but his reaction was one of abject humility and apology, and it allowed her some other options for her sake and her kids. She backed off of the divorce demand, but he clearly needed a significant repentance plan. They developed a very robust plan that could allow the marriage to heal. However, if he won't fully participate in the plan, then the marriage will most likely be over.

One of the purposes of repentance plans is to provide a pathway to restore a relationship rather than just submit to hurtful behavior or throw away the relationship. In every relationship, change is needed. A repentance plan is a way to introduce the needed change so the relationship can go forward.

Think of it as an agreement of what you will do or what they get to do to you if you do this offense again. I have seen people doing dishes for a month as a part of a repentance plan. I have seen people coming home in the middle of the day to make the bed or close the shower curtain. I have seen people buying gifts for the offended person. The idea is for there to be a way of developing, growing, and even punishing for repeated sins in particular areas. John the Baptist suspected that some religious people were just faking their repentance, so he told them that he wanted to see fruit in keeping with their repentance (Luke 3:8).

Repentance plans can be for small offenses but are mandatory for deeply offensive or repetitive behaviors. What if a person has been sober for years but goes back to the bottle? What if a person is very cruel in their sarcasm, and it destroys the safety of the home? What if a person repeatedly views pornography? These might be times for lengthy visits away from the family. It could be time for a rehab stay. It could be working on an unpleasant project.

Be realistic about repentance plans, though—they need to be tough enough so that the person thinks twice about repeating the offense. There must be ways short of divorce where both parties can direct change into the relationship.

I realize this idea may sound different, maybe even harsh, but it is important for couples to have small and big ways to say, "Please respect me on this; it hurts." I have watched too many couples who don't have ways of letting each other know of the hurts that come up in marriage. They just pile up and pile up until one day one spouse has had enough and they leave. It doesn't have to be this way. Find a way to let your spouse have some corrective power in your life and watch your relationship improve.

Step Six: Test for openness.

The last action is to test for openness. When we hurt another person, they close up towards us. It is a natural and instinctive reaction. If someone consistently hurts us, we begin to shut down towards them. If we are going to have a ridiculously great marriage, then both people must be as open as possible towards one another. When the apology is effective, the wounded person will open back up towards the person who has hurt them.

This is the test: Are they willing to talk with you or let you touch them? If they will not let you touch them or talk with you about other topics, the issue is likely not resolved yet. We are like flowers and open up to the people we trust. The key issue is *trust*. An apology is designed to reestablish trust between two people. If I feel like you get it, I can trust you again. If you don't really understand and you just want to move on, or even worse, you pretend that what you did was not hurtful, then trust is severely damaged. After an effective apology, some level of trust has been reestablished. This trust can be measured through whether you will talk with me and/or if you will let me touch you. If you won't do either of these, then something is wrong. I need to start the apology process over again. If you are going to have a great marriage, you need openness—there needs to be trust.

Let me say this again. You will offend your spouse, so get used to apologizing. You will hurt your spouse, so be ready with an admission of your guilt. Your spouse will be offended by things you don't do and things you do, so practice apologizing. Have the kind of marriage where "I was wrong," "I apologize," "I am sorry," and so forth, are regular phrases that go back and forth between you as a couple. Do not expect your spouse to be perfect. Do not pretend you are perfect either.

If you struggle to understand where you've gone wrong, it helps to look at the basic three relational problems:

Have I failed to do something I should have done?

Have I done something I shouldn't have done?

Have I harmed my spouse or family in some way?

Almost all of the ways to damage a relationship are a variation of one of these three. Be willing to listen to your spouse about these. Let the apology process become a staple in your marriage.

Express Every Positive, Every Time

How many times do you think to yourself, "My wife is so incredibly beautiful"? Or "I'm so lucky to have a husband who loves me for me"? I bet a lot! But do you say the actual words you're thinking? This little habit is a game-changer in building a welcoming, positive environment for your marriage to dwell in. It is the act of expressing the positive thoughts or feelings you hold for your spouse—*every time* you have them. Yes, *every time*. And while this may seem extreme, I promise your spouse needs and wants to hear from you about all the positives he or she is doing. We can't ever give or get enough honest, positive feedback. Do not let moments of joy, love, connection, or delight slide by. Let your spouse know all the positive feelings you have about them regularly and often.

The Bible is clear on the idea that both husbands and wives need to receive value from each other (Eph. 5:25–33; 1 Pet. 3:7–9). This is really true for all relationships but especially in marriage. When we are in a relationship with another person, there has to be a mutual acknowledgment of how valuable the other person is. When we don't, we begin to take their positives for granted and only focus on the negatives. Don't let that happen. Mention the positives, think about the positives, force yourself to notice the positives.

We need our partner to acknowledge all the good things we are doing, too, so we don't sink into the background. Without this habit, we don't really know where we stand with the other person, which can really strain things. It's interesting that by extolling the other person's value to us, it actually adds to our own value. This is so powerful and often overlooked.

One way I keep my marriage alive and vibrant is that I tell my wife every night a number of the positive things I noticed about her that day. I send her a text after she has gone to bed thanking her for all she did that day. This focuses my mind on noticing the positives. Let me give you a window into a text exchange between me and my wife. Ask yourself if this kind of positive interaction would help your marriage.

From Gil to Dana one night:

> What a pleasure to have a normal dinner and evening on the couch watching TV with you. Of course, I love everything shared with you. I am so very encouraged with all of the things that you do. I think it is great that you are looking at taking more control over your Pilates work. I am encouraged that you did not pack your schedule today so you had no room for a real day off. I thank you for the wonderful salad and the work on the budget and keeping it up to date. I hope that this note finds you extremely well rested as another gift of God's grace. I am excited about the chance to get away with you next week and enjoy So Cal. What a treat. This summer is working out so well. Thank you for all the work that you are putting in to make it all a reality...your hard work at your job...the planning of the various vacations...the money to our daughter...the laundry...the groceries... the relationships with the girls...and most of all, still having time for me. I so value your listening to my day and telling me about your day. Every day and every week we keep making progress because of you. I love you and find your soul and your body irresistibly alluring.

From Dana to Gil a few nights later:

> Thank you for noticing me and appreciating what I do. I love listening to you and value the trust you have in me to share. I'm also grateful for the life we have, our peaceful relationship with each other and our girls. I am immensely grateful for all the answered prayers. Thank you for praying for me. God encouraged me today with the thought to "depend on His presence, His plan, His promises, and His help in every situation. And that I'm to carry that comfort to the hurting people in my midst." Can't wait to see what the day brings. I love you and look forward to another night together.

From Gil to Dana on a different night:

> What a lovely time going to the movie tonight. You are such a wonderful date. Thank you for going out with me. Not every man gets such a lovely and interesting woman to date each week. I do and I never want to take that for granted. I loved hearing about your

work day. It is great that _____ and you are getting more collegial. You are breezing through these days which once caused heart palpitations. Thank you for hanging in there and making all of this work for yourself, Grace, us, and your patients...let alone the breath of fresh air you are to your colleagues. I must thank you profusely for all the work you did to make my trip to the DMV a real positive and easy experience. They had all the electronic records. You had put together all of the things that I needed and I breezed through it. Thank you, thank you, thank you. Thank you for allowing me to talk about, pray about, and explore all the new possibilities that people bring to me, even the ones that you know are crazy and would significantly damage our family if I were to really do them. It is very healing that you can hear them and not immediately shut them down because they are stupid or threatening. I am a very fortunate man to be married to a woman who can listen to her husband bring his crazy ideas and allow him to think his way through them all. You are a rare gift to me. Thank you.

As a pastor who talks to hundreds of couples each year about their marriage, one of the worst statements I hear is, "I feel taken for granted." When I hear this, it clues me into the fact that the couple needs to work on this particular habit in the relationship. One couple I know almost got divorced because the husband never told his wife about all the wonderful thoughts and feelings he had about her, which were many. His wife was starving for affection and ready to leave. He always bragged to everyone else about how wonderful she was, but he never told her. Fortunately, I was able to convince him to start verbalizing all the joyful and loving things he said to me about her. It was a pivotal moment for their relationship—the marriage turned around.

Let me help you see this another way by using the workplace as an example. A number of studies have been done about employees. In every study where appreciation is increased, productivity and worker morale always go up. Employers often think their employees do not need verbal appreciation so much because they get a good salary and benefits. But no. The vast majority of people at work do not feel appreciated for all they do at work. The best work places are consistently where people feel valued and significant for the contribution they make. Making others feel appreciated and significant can change a workplace. If this is the case at work where people get a salary and benefits, imagine the difference it can make in a marriage.

Think about your own marriage for a moment. Both of you are sort of like employees who work for the other person, for the family, for the greater good of the marriage entity. Neither of you earns any money doing this, but the purpose behind the work is to produce something far more valuable than money—love, connection, belonging, safety, relationship, and solid, healthy kids. Whenever you or your spouse do something good toward what is needed, they should be acknowledged and appreciated, because like employees, you are both in need of affirmation.

In this chapter, I think you'll find it helpful to write down your thoughts. Getting things down on paper rather than just thinking it to yourself works wonders. I've provided a few writing prompts and some space to write, or you can transfer your answers to a journal or notebook. Right now, consider your spouse. What are five things you specifically appreciate about him or her? Write them down here:

1.

2.

3.

4.

5.

Now, plan to tell your spouse one of these affirming things within the next day or two. Better yet, do it now. Send a text, make a call, leave a voice message, send an email, or even post it on social media (if it won't embarrass them).

Keep Your Marriage Positive

Great marriages stay positive. I can bet there has never been a great marriage where the partners were negative, sarcastic, and angry at each other for long stretches of time. Sure we can get frustrated or even mad at our spouse, but couples in great marriages don't allow themselves to stay in that negative place for long. If every couple forced themselves back to a positive view of their spouse, eventually they would create a ridiculously great marriage.

Remember when you were dating? All of the negative things that took place during the dating phase are probably still present in your current relationship. But back then, you were so enamored with each other you didn't focus on them. Instead, you both focused on the positive elements of one other and built each other up. This undoubtedly made the relationship delightful for both of you, enough so that you wanted to spend the rest of your life together.

Now that you're married, it is way too easy to see all the weaknesses and selfishness in your spouse. We all have negatives, but if you let those obvious problems dominate your thinking, the marriage will suffer. Difficult, even tragic, things will come crashing into your marriage, so you have to figure out a way to be positive about each other and your relationship at all times. Yes, I know that not everything about your marriage or your situation is always positive, but if you constantly dwell on those negative things, it will damage the relationship. I've seen it happen time and again. Acknowledge the negative and find the solution but focus on the positive in that person.

I remember working with one couple where the wife was constantly disappointed in her husband. Her focus was either on what he was not doing or what he was doing wrong. He should do this, he should have done that, he should know that this needs to be done, and so on. I eventually asked her if these were things she would know to do if she were in his position. She said, "Of course!" So (cautiously) I said, "You are really criticizing your husband for not being you. You realize, of course, that he is a different person, and God gave him different gifts, a distinct temperament, and unique experiences."

This dose of reality was a light-bulb moment for her. Her husband was a wonderful man, a wonderful husband, and a great father in so many ways, but she had stopped seeing those things; instead, she was laser-focused on what he was not doing that she would know to do. When she started to force her gaze to the good things he was doing, she began to see more and more of his good things. He blossomed even more under her praise and appreciation. This new positive focus turned their marriage around from one that was headed to divorce court to a delightful blend of two different people.

There is a principle in life that says, "What you look for you see." And I would like to add, "What you look for you will get more of!" Don't doom your marriage to a negative death-spiral. Focus on the good, the positive, and the improving. Let your spouse know that you notice all of it—the good, the effort made, the positive, the helpful. He or she is a work in progress just as you are, and both of you will give more of what is praised and appreciated.

Now I am assuming that you would improve your marriage if you could all on your own, but what you really want is your partner to change and they are not changing. So work on the things you can control—appreciating your spouse for everything, but especially any movement in the direction that would be helpful in your marriage. Change the mood in your relationship by rehearsing things like your spouse's good points, the positive elements in your marriage, and your family's helpful elements. It is amazing how much can change when the oil of appreciation, praise, and sincere gratitude is applied.

Consider five positive things about your life as it relates to your spouse, marriage, or family. Write them down here:

1.

2.

3.

4.

5.

Let me just say this again. *Great marriages stay positive.* This doesn't mean couples with great marriages haven't gone through difficulties or had arguments, but it does mean that if you want a ridiculously great marriage, you will emphasize the good, the positive, and the redeeming aspects of your relationship. Yes, your spouse is less than perfect, and so are you. But unless your spouse is immorally criminal, there is *always* hope for your relationship. Get over the fact that you are married to a less-than-perfect person. Stay focused on the positive.

There might be many things your spouse is not doing or things they are negatively doing that are damaging the relationship. But if you are not careful, your attention will be riveted on just the negative and you will think, "I can't be positive until this thing changes." Do not let your focus be on those things. Focus on what they do well—on what they bring to the relationship. Instead of going negative, you can work a different process. Focus on why they are a good person. Don't just think to yourself, "They already know I think this is great." *Say it.* Most people in our world are starved for affection and encouragement. Spouses should be each other's greatest source of encouragement.

What are five strengths of your spouse or things you admire about him or her? How can you encourage your spouse today? Write them here:

1.

2.

3.

4.

5.

BUILDING A DELIGHTFUL ENVIRONMENT

I've mentioned this before, but one of the greatest realizations each couple must come to is that the marriage is a separate entity apart from the individual man and woman in the marriage. Seems basic, but marriages get into trouble all the time when the two individuals lose touch with this reality.

This separate thing—this marriage—is built through the words you say, the actions you do, the attitudes you emote, and the thoughts you think. The more positive you are about your relationship, the more positive the relationship will be. Negativity breeds a negative environment. Assuming you want a delightful environment to dwell in, the two of you can literally create a positive environment for you both to dwell in by all the positive, helpful, and encouraging things you say and do. This ties in with kindness in habit #3. There will always be negatives that want to dominate your attention and spoil the way you think about your spouse. Don't let them. Instead, remain positive about the good things in your spouse's life, and be positive about the *goodness* of the relationship. The more kind, positive words, actions, and attitudes relayed between you and your spouse, the better the relational environment.

Think of this concept like a huge air conditioner. When the air conditioner kicks on during a hot day, it seems like this little delightful breeze of cool air will not do much good in the whole house; but over time, the continual flow of cool air from the air conditioner causes the whole temperature to change.

Don't we all want to be a part of a relationship where 98 percent of the time we get warmth, acceptance, and love? Or in the case of the air-conditioner example, refreshment, delight, and relief? Don't we all move away from negative people and relationships? They are very hard to be around for too much time! Make your marriage something that you and your partner want to move toward. Be positive. Don't keep the positive thoughts to yourself.

This might be strange for you starting out, but do it anyway. You don't have to worry about praising people too much as long as your praises are tied to a specific action or quality they are exhibiting. It only takes one of you to begin, so let it be with you. Your spouse might wonder what has come over you or what you want from them, but your answer will always be, "Nothing. I just appreciate you." You want them to know all the positive things you think and feel about them. All the ways you delight in them.

And tell them as specifically as you can, such as:

I like how hard you work.

I like how great that meal was.

I was just delighted watching you take out the trash.

I was so overwhelmed with joy watching you work with the kids.

I really like the way you look right now.

I appreciate that you would let me purchase this thing I want.

I was just thinking back on the time we did _____, and it made me so happy.

You are incredible with the finances.

You are amazing that you can figure out the kids' school schedules.

Have I told you recently that I think you are terrific for my soul?

I look at you and see a great provider, thanks.

I look at you and appreciate that you speak so kindly to me when I know you may want to yell, thanks.

Thank you for going to work every day. You work so hard for us.

I love the fact that you are so conscientious at work.

Look at who you are becoming: _____

The journey we are on has been wonderful, thank you.

You don't just have to tell them these things verbally—you can write a note and leave it in their lunch bag; you can give them a gift; you can take a picture or text them a meme—get creative! These little positive elements are incredibly powerful in building a welcoming, positive environment for your relationship. Do this at least once a day. Don't let a day go by that you do not add to the positivity of your relationship.

This is so simple that people miss it, especially during good times. You will have dozens of joyful and positive thoughts about your spouse. Don't just think or feel them and say nothing. Let the other person know at that moment. The rule of thumb is this: every time you have a positive, encouraging, or loving thought about your spouse, let them know—*every time.*

The last thing I want you to write down are the five greatest reasons for being in a relationship with your spouse. These are the five things that can serve as reminders about why you chose to do life with this person. For me, my wife makes me a much better person. Let me give you part of my extensive list of why she is so wonderful, what I would write if I were filling this out.

1. My wife is incredibly intelligent; she is wonderfully responsible; she is so flexible and adaptable.

2. She is gorgeous and works at staying beautiful.

3. She is unbelievably perseverant, lovingly complimentary and insightful, and she makes our house a pleasant and delightful home. She is incredibly easy to be with.

4. She listens to all my ideas, points of view, and crazy dreams. She is way more supportive of me than she should be, and she is willing to sacrifice for the good of our marriage and our family.

5. She is discreet and protective, and she steps in where I am not talented, gifted, or able. She understands my needs and works hard to meet them even if they don't connect to her needs.

Now it's your turn.

Enjoy this process—your spouse is amazing. Give yourself time to think and write down all of the ways.

1.

2.

3.

4.

5.

Seek Wisdom, Not Your Own Way

One day, I was watching a couple fight over their different perspectives on furniture for their kitchen. Let's call them Javon and Stephanie. They both staked out their positions and neither was budging. Javon didn't want to spend more money on a kitchen table because the one they had was perfectly fine. Stephanie insisted they needed a new table that would reflect her style and decor choices. They were both sending missiles at the other person for not being reasonable.

Tragically enough, this argument is what eventually caused the wife to declare she could not live with this man—she divorced him! This was a tragic ending to a common problem. They were seeking their own way instead of wisdom. It didn't have to be that way. What could have saved this marriage? I believe they could have implemented this next habit—*seek wisdom, not your own way*. You see, Javon and Stephanie didn't understand a solution was at hand only by acknowledging the wisdom of their partner's position. Both people had specific reasons for their viewpoints, but there was no willingness to listen, understand, compromise, or even look for other options.

I have found that when people disagree over anything, it is best if they stop and tell themselves they are on a quest for wisdom not their way. Many people feel that unless they get exactly what they want, the other person has won and it is a loss for them. This is a very binary way of thinking. Marriage is not a competition between two partners. If one person loses, you both lose and the marriage loses. We must constantly look for the action, decision, and words that allow everyone to win.

This is where wisdom lives.

To find wisdom, we must be willing to get past this binary thinking, past a self-focus, and search for it wherever it may come from. The process of finding wisdom usually requires multiple conversations, looking for facts, checking with others, consideration of new information, allowing time to absorb new perspectives, and a willingness to be flexible. This is a purposeful, deliberate habit that can help keep the fights from becoming overwhelming and vicious.

Recently, my wife and I were discussing a possible vacation we could take. We wanted to tie it to a business trip she wanted to make, and it did sound exciting. Even better, it would be partly tax deductible! My initial reaction internally was we couldn't afford it, which must have leaked out on my face because she reacted to my negative tone. Instead of responding to her reaction by pushing back or insisting on my way, I told myself, "We are looking for wisdom, not just my way." Doing this completely changed the mood. Instead of shutting her down, we explored all the possibilities. It was great talking about how much fun it could be, all the things we could do, and how much she would benefit professionally.

Knowing my budget concerns were legitimate, I suggested finding alternatives to keep the costs down. By morning, my wife had done a complete workup of all the expenses for the two possibilities we talked about the night before. But she also added two more possibilities that we hadn't known about. Her analysis was brilliant and would allow us to both save money and accomplish all we wanted it to. Together, we were finding wisdom.

Seeking wisdom, not your own way is one of the vital habits for a ridiculously great marriage. It requires a subtle, but crucial, shift of attitude that says:

> "I don't have to defend my position or bash the other person's position. My first idea is just my initial opinion and will not necessarily be what I think in the long-term when all the facts and multiple perspectives are known. Together, we are seeking wisdom, and when we do the research and explore all the options, it will be clear what we should do."

When we come into each discussion with the idea that we are open to wisdom from wherever it comes from, we will recognize it when it arrives. Our open attitude toward alternative perspectives and ideas allows us to see wise ideas and not be closed off to truly brilliant options.

WHAT IS THE WISE DECISION?

Making a wise decision is not a fast-track approach. It can take time, patience, and resources to come to the wise plan. But to know what a wise decision even looks like, we have to do three things: define what wisdom is, know its source, and develop an approach to go after it.

The definition of wisdom is *practical knowledge that works to bring about a win for everyone in the situation*. That includes a win for not only you and your spouse but God as well, since He is the source of all wisdom and willing to share it (Prov. 2:6; Is. 55:9; Jas. 1:5). I call it the triple-win: God has to win; the other person has to win; you have to win. I believe there is always a triple-win possibility in every situation. It is not always obvious at first or easy to accommodate, but it is always there. The book of Proverbs is a brilliant collection of godly wisdom for all kinds of situations in life. Solomon says if we are going to find wisdom, we must cry out for it and search for her as if for silver. Notice how Proverbs 2:2–11 says we must commit to searching for wisdom or else we will not find it:

> *Make your ear attentive to wisdom,*
>
> *Incline your heart to understanding;*
>
> *For if you cry for discernment,*
>
> *Lift your voice for understanding;*
>
> *If you seek her as silver*
>
> *And search for her as for hidden treasures;*
>
> *Then you will discern the fear of the Lord*
>
> *And discover the knowledge of God.*
>
> *For the Lord gives wisdom;*
>
> *From His mouth come knowledge and understanding.*
>
> *He stores up sound wisdom for the upright;*
>
> *He is a shield to those who walk in integrity,*
>
> *Guarding the paths of justice,*
>
> *And He preserves the way of His godly ones.*
>
> *Then you will discern righteousness and justice*
>
> *And equity and every good course.*
>
> *For wisdom will enter your heart*

And knowledge will be pleasant to your soul;

Discretion will guard you,

Understanding will watch over you.

In other words, the first thought you have on a subject is not naturally the full measure of wisdom; seeking is necessary to find a solution for everyone to win. You may have one aspect of wisdom, but it may not be a win for everyone. Start by recognizing that fact and then keep searching. Go after the wise solution; pursue it.

Pursuing the Wise Solution

Great couples are willing to admit to themselves and each other that they don't know everything. Each partner welcomes the advice, input, and insights from their spouse knowing it will help them as a couple to make a better decision overall. And while God is the source of all wisdom, He gives us all kinds of great resources for wisdom, one being the Bible, but there are plenty of people who are wise too. They host websites, blogs, books, seminars, and so forth, that will very likely provide wise answers and feedback for your specific issue. Both of you can do your homework for the benefit of the other. (Also see ptlb. com/breakfast-with-solomon.)

Before my wife and I ever have a serious discussion, I say to myself and many times to her, "There are always options." "These are only ideas." "I do not have all the wisdom." This reminds us that everyone's point is valid and we don't know all there is to know on the subject. Sometimes we divvy up the research that is needed. She is going to talk to so-and-so; I'm going to find some articles about it, and so on. The point is that we both seek wisdom not just our own way. We keep listening. We keep trying various options and combinations until we find the wise solution.

We need to build on the perspectives of both people in the marriage. One way we show our spouse that we value his or her ideas is to consider how they were raised or taught or trained. What do they value the most? Do they have more experience or expertise in an area? What do they see as the end goal to strive for? What is at the heart of their request? What is their motivation, true worry, or concern? How would they spend the money and why? Is there a way to do both things? Is there someone we should talk to who could help us see this problem from a different angle?

DEALING WITH STRONG PERSONALITIES

The marriages with the least amount of joy and the least amount of excitement are the ones where one person dominates the other with their opinions, ideas, plans, and points of view. If both people are not present in the marriage, it is not a dynamic relationship. Whoever has the stronger personality (this could be the man or the woman) tends to get their own point across with little regard or patience for the other one's needs. The caution here is for the spouse with the strong personality. Promoting your ideas as the only way to go can come with destructive consequences. If your spouse feels undermined by your dominance, or if their sense of well-being is crushed by your constant need to express your opinion, then the relationship is diminished. The answer or solution or choice isn't as important as the process of finding the win for everyone. If you get your own way but you've alienated or hurt your spouse, then no one has won.

Some people I work with have no idea they have caused any hurt by using the power of their personality to constantly get their way. They're so busy trying to get their own way, they haven't noticed the lack of real relationship with their partner. If your spouse is withdrawn and isn't as quick to contribute to decisions or plans that need to be made, or perhaps your spouse consistently acquiesces without giving their point of view, then you may be overpowering your partner with your personality. Another possibility is that your partner does what they want without consulting you at all. This is a more passive-aggressive approach. These are all signs that your spouse feels ignored or their opinions and ideas don't matter.

Your spouse just may not have the energy to fight for what he or she wants, so they either give in easily or do the thing they want to do anyway but without you. The stronger person must work hard to draw out the less vocal person. If the marriage is to truly be a ridiculously great relationship, then both people must contribute their wisdom.

Remember, you are in this together. I have watched too many men and women who try and win against their spouse and then wonder why their marriage is so troubled. If I am upset at the fact that my leg is hurting and I stab my leg with a knife, I have not helped myself. We don't win if we make our spouse miserable. The goal is a win-win-win for God, you, and your spouse.

THE WISE WAY MAY REQUIRE PATIENCE

I can remember watching with pleasure how Don and Rebecca lived a delightful marriage. Rebecca was a risk taker and an exceptional leader. Her husband, Don, was an organizer and much quieter than his wife. She often suggested some risky things, and instead of pushing away her ideas, he would have discussions with her about how they could pull them off. Her ideas made sense to her, and yes, they stretched their marriage and finances; but her ideas also allowed them to move into great positions financially while keeping their love alive. If Don had refused to even consider what Rebecca was suggesting, their marriage and lives would likely have been small and negative. But because both of them sought to find the win for each other and for God, their marriage and lives kept expanding.

Tell yourself, "I am seeking wisdom, not my own way." Listen to what your spouse is saying. Have a "Let's-look-at-that-as-a-possibility" mindset. Suggest a fact sheet on paper with costs, possibilities, options, and research. Give yourself all the time you can to find new points of view and do the actual research. The process of finding wisdom will take several conversations. It will require work and time to talk, read, discuss, and listen. Realize your spouse is bringing this idea to you because it makes sense to them. So ask yourself, "Why does this make sense to them?" Try to understand their perspective.

Sometimes the wise solution takes a while to see. If the solution is delayed, wise couples will wait until wisdom is revealed. There have been many times when my original position has needed to be completely abandoned or significantly modified because of something Dana has said or something we have learned as we began to look for wisdom. We work to find the solution together. If both of you agree that you are going after wisdom, then it will present itself to one or both of you. Ask:

> *How am I demonstrating that I am seeking wisdom not my own way?*
>
> *How can I show my spouse in obvious ways that I am open to wisdom and not just seeking my own way?*
>
> *What articles can we read?*
>
> *Who can we talk to?*
>
> *What programs will help us?*
>
> *What real-life situation or facts can help us see a different perspective?*
>
> *How will we make this a triple-win?*

If you are going after your own way, there will most likely be a fight. Be willing to listen. Be willing to seek. And be willing to be patient with the answer if a wise solution isn't forthcoming. Don't be afraid to delay the decision until you can do more research, talk to more people, or pray.

Habit #7

Pray Individually and Together

Couples who enjoy ridiculously great marriages develop their spiritual lives, as well as all the other habits. I want to suggest this next habit to do just that—*pray individually and together*. Connecting yourself to God strengthens your marriage in so many ways. Praying together for various parts of your life opens a soul connection between two people that is not possible any other way. In this habit, you will add two small windows of time to your day—one for your own spiritual connection to God, and one to connect the two of you together with God.

SPEND TIME WITH GOD PERSONALLY EVERY DAY

Let me give you a simple way to spend time with God every day. I call it the C.H.R.I.S.T. method. Many people are interested in having God speak to them personally, and these little spiritual exercises will allow God to engage with you. It will take between five and thirty minutes a day to make connection with God and interact with Him about your day. Here is how the C.H.R.I.S.T. acronym can work for you.

C = **Confession.** Get in a quiet place or quiet mental space and ask God if there are any ways that you have displeased Him in the last twenty-four hours. If He brings up something, then ask Him to forgive it through the love and sacrifice of Jesus Christ on the cross. Thank Him for forgiving you and ask Him to give you strength and direction so you won't do that selfish action in the future.

H = **Holy Spirit.** Open your Bible to a particular book, like Philippians or James or Proverbs, and ask God the Holy Spirit to show you what He wants you to know from the Scriptures for that day or the next day (if you do this at night). If you read slowly through a portion of the Bible—listening, praying, and thinking of your concerns—God will answer you through the Scriptures.

R = Repetition. When God the Holy Spirit directs you to a particular passage or phrase in Scripture, start studying that section and read it over and over, asking God to show you how to understand and apply that particular passage to your life. You may want to look up the words in the dictionary, check other passages in the Bible that have the same idea, and even look up a commentary to make sure you are interpreting the passage rightly. God speaks through His Word, and the more we read and repeat it, the more we understand what He is trying to tell us.

I = Interaction. This is where you talk with God about the concerns you have and ask Him for the things you need for yourself and hope God will do for others. It truly is an interaction with God about what He said to you in Scripture. It is also about what is happening in your life and the positive and negative changes He wants you to make.

S = Service. Ask God if there is a way you can serve Him in the next day or so. It may be to help a particular person. It may be to volunteer to help a worthy cause. It may be to love one of the people already in your life in a new way. God wants His love to flow through us and He will send us on adventures to encourage and bless others.

T = Togetherness. This means that weekly we need to spend time with other Christians worshipping God and talking with them about how God is working in us. There is something very fulfilling and developmental about worshipping with a group of sincere believers and having them know how you are really doing in your life.

I have been helping Christians do these things every day for a long time. I often find that it is not until a man or a woman reconnects with God in a growing way that their marriage changes. The spiritual dimension of our lives is a very dynamic aspect of our being. When we open the dynamism of God in our life again, a new joy can flood into the marriage.

PRAYING TOGETHER EVERY NIGHT

Praying together is one of the most intimate things next to sex a couple can do together. To have a ridiculously great marriage, spending a few minutes at the end of the day praying together as a husband and wife pays rich dividends. It is one of those hidden practices couples can do that invites God's power into the relationship. It doesn't have to be long (it could only be sixty seconds), but opening up this spiritual dimension in the marriage is vital. Yes, one spouse may be much further along in their faith than the other, but you can still enjoy growing deeper spiritually together. The important thing is to pray even if one spouse doesn't say anything right away.

Praying while your spouse sits quietly with head bowed or eyes closed can be just as enjoyable and beneficial to both of your spiritual lives. And I think you'll find, eventually, he or she will begin to say a few words. Just make sure to pause so they can get a word in if they feel led to speak. Also, don't make it so long that the other person is bored out of their mind while you pray. Maybe squeeze their hand as a signal you're pausing to allow them to speak if they want to. It is important to pray by yourself, but it's crucial to pray together too. You might have heard this saying, "Couples who pray together, stay together." I certainly tend to think so. That's because when a couple prays together, they are going to God directly for specific things in their life expecting to see Him answer those needs or work in a situation.

Another reason why it is great to pray together daily is to hear your spouse's heart. At first, it may take a few days or even a few weeks for either spouse to realize they are talking to God rather than trying to score points with their spouse. But eventually, the true heart begins to show. Both spouses will be able to hear the other's heart and their deep cries for help and wisdom. When couples let their guard down a little in prayer, it can be very healing.

It is not enough to know why we should pray; we have to actually do it. I have seen prayer help so many families, so I am going to get detailed about ways to pray together. Hopefully, this will be helpful to you. If you have good ideas of how to pray together that are different from mine, wonderful! But if you have not started or have been inconsistent with praying together, these ideas may help. You can also check out several prayer resources I have written over the years, including *Touching the Heart of God, Spiritual Disciplines of a C.H.R.I.S.T.I.A.N.* and *Going Deep in Prayer.*

GUIDELINES FOR PRAYING TOGETHER

It is important for both people to be active participants in the prayer time. You'll both want to suggest prayer items, maybe even write down the prayers in a prayer journal and how God has answered them. Both people don't have to pray out loud, but they must both be active in the prayer. Address God and let your spouse also address Him. The opening of your soul in talking with God allows your spouse to experience another dimension of your person. In my marriage, I do most of the praying out loud, but I have seen some wonderful couples where the wife does the majority of the talking. Either way, spend time together with God.

First, start by setting a standard time. Scheduling time to pray together is a lot easier than you realize. Before either of you goes to bed, pray together. If one person turns in before the other one, spend a few minutes before they turn out the lights praying. Don't let your spouse go to bed without prayer time. Some couples find that praying together in the morning is better for them. Great! I also encourage couples to pray before they leave the house. Some families even incorporate it into the morning ritual. This means, though, that you have to be ahead of schedule and incorporate it into the morning. It's easy to get sidetracked by distractions. If you don't work at it and plan for it, something will always keep you from praying.

Second, find a good place to pray. This can be in bed, the bathroom, or some other place in the house where praying is comfortable. You can pray in any number of positions...kneeling, standing, sitting, lying face down. Find a common position or place and pray for a few minutes every night as you head off to sleep. Do whatever works best for both of you, and do it every day.

Many nights, I will sit in one of my favorite chairs and my wife will stand behind me leaning on the back of the chair. We pray for each other, our girls, and our friends. We always ask that God will cover us under the blood of the Lord Jesus Christ and the power of the Holy Spirit. We ask for God to strengthen us and minister to us while we sleep, and to be His agents the next day. We ask that we would be discerning and wise in the decisions we need to make the next day or in the near future.

Some nights, my wife and I pray lying on the bed or sitting in a chair near the bed. If my wife goes to bed early (and I am planning to stay up later), I will stand or kneel next to her bedside and pray with her.

Third, keep it brief but complete. Prayer time doesn't have to take long, but sometimes it might, depending on what is going on in your lives and with the people you love. It would be better if the prayer time isn't long and drawn out—after all, it is at the end of the day and you are both probably tired. I don't even mind if my wife falls asleep with me praying; it comforts her, and I'm okay with that.

I will generally pray about our kids, the things they are going through, and what we hope is the right resolution of these things. I will pray for our friends and the people who we know who have particular burdens that need to be taken before the Lord. We will pray for specific actions God can take into the life of these people. We are always open to what God might prompt us to ask Him to do in the life of a particular family member or friend.

PRAYER GUIDES

A prayer guide is a sort of map to help you through prayer time. In fact, throughout church history, people have used prayer guides to keep them focused and moving forward in the prayer. The key to people being able to pray for more than a few sentences is to have a prayer guide that moves you through topics, ideas, and issues you would not normally consider. I find having specifics to pray for is encouraging and helps us to pray consistently. I have several I use for my personal time with God, but for our prayer time together, we use a variety of guides depending on how much time or energy we have on that given night. Feel free to borrow these as a guide or create your own.

Bedtime prayer guide:

Thank God for what He has done that day or week.

Ask Him for blessings, protection, love, and direction for each member of the immediate family.

Ask Him for specific blessings, protection, love, and direction for friends and relatives.

Ask Him for protection during sleeping and His energy for tomorrow.

People-based guide:

Spouse—*ask them what they want to pray about or need prayer for.*

Family—*the immediate members as well as the future ones.*

Friends—*what they need not just what they want.*

Church—*initiatives and programs that need to be covered in prayer at your church.*

Acquaintances—*those people God has moved into your life that day or week.*

Nation—*morality, civility, political courage, leadership, and so forth.*

Spirit-based guide:

Protection—*for God to surround you and keep temptations, attacks, and obstacles from you, especially if you know one is coming.*

Guidance—*that God would make it clear what His will is for you, your spouse, and family.*

Growth—*for areas and opportunities where you or your family need to grow.*

Love—*for love to overflow into your life as you sleep and throughout the day tomorrow.*

Needs—*friends and relatives who have asked you to pray for them or you feel some burden to ask things from God—whatever God puts on your heart to pray for yourself and the people in your family.*

Sample prayer:

Dear Heavenly Father,

We come in the name of the Lord Jesus, and we thank you for all the things you have done for us today. Thank you for (at least three things that happened that day).

We ask that you would inject your love, grace, and mercy into our lives while we are sleeping and while we go about our day tomorrow.

We need you to pursue us and meet our needs (mention some of your needs).

We need you to give us more than we deserve of your power, gifts, and direction (mention specifically what His power in you could do).

We need you to give us your mercy. We know that we are sinners and we are guilty of pride, envy, anger, lust, sloth, gluttony, and greed. Thank you for forgiving us for our sins in Christ Jesus.

We ask you for your blessings to enrich our lives (ask God for at least three blessings that would make your life more righteous, loving, and kind).

We need your guidance for our decisions. Show us what to do even if it is different from what we have always done (talk to God about the decisions you are facing).

Here is an example of how to pray for others:

I pray for my spouse that you would…

I ask, Lord, that you would minister to our children...

I ask, Lord, to open the eyes of our friends to see.... and make new choices...

I pray, Lord, that Bill, who I met today, is able to see a new perspective or...

I pray that you would give Dad lots of friends and joy as he lives in retirement...

I ask that I would have courage and wisdom in my new work assignment...

I pray for the Holy Spirit to fill me with your love for the people I will encounter tomorrow.

I do ask, Lord Jesus, that you would cover (names of your immediate family members) under the blood of the Lord Jesus Christ and the power of the Holy Spirit in every part of their spirit, soul, and body so the enemy will not have any means of attacking, oppressing, or afflicting us tonight or tomorrow.

As Christians, our strongest protection comes from the life, death, and resurrection of Jesus Christ and the Holy Spirit sent to guide us.

In Christ's Name we pray,

Amen

Adding this simple, impactful habit to the end of your day deepens your marriage relationship in a way few things can. The more you do this, the more comfortable you will become talking with God in front of your spouse. Some of the masks will come down and a whole new dimension of who you are will come into view. It will make your marriage much richer and more enjoyable—more ridiculous. Make it happen every night as genuinely as you can in a repeatable way and just watch what happens.

Don't make it super complicated—just pray together. Don't make the time too formal either. My wife, after she has prayed at the beginning of the prayer time, regularly falls asleep during my prayers at night because I get going in prayer for the children, friends, or the church. This is okay, and it has become a wonderful part of our bedtime ritual. Did you stay awake while I was praying above?

Talk with your spouse and come up with your own prayer plan:

> *Will you commit to praying together every night?*
>
> *When will you pray together? Night time? Morning? Lunch?*
>
> *Where will prayer time be most comfortable or accessible?*
>
> *How will you conduct prayer time? Who will lead?*
>
> *Will you use a guide? Will you keep a prayer journal?*

Habit #8

Schedule Intimacy

Great couples schedule sex. Scheduled sex? How unromantic! But really, this is a major key to a ridiculously great marriage. Making time for sexual activity does not take away any of the romance from the marriage; rather, it makes it purposeful and focused. Too many couples wait for both people to feel like it, but this is not the way to handle this crucial element in your marriage. It leads to too little sex and, very likely, unmet needs for one or both partners.

Planning time for intimacy is another essential habit to master. You and your spouse plan to have dinner at a certain time each night, right? So, plan when you are going to have sex and what kind of sex it will be. (I'll explain the three general kinds of sex below.) My hope is to bring a huge level of sexual satisfaction to your marriage instead of frustration.

There are lots of issues to cover, but this one habit, if implemented well, will *significantly* reduce tension in many marriages. Scheduling intimacy can be somewhat complicated, as it has to account for physical needs, sexual desires, schedules, and whether you have other people living with you or not (children, guests, and so forth). But the key is making sex a priority.

In most marriages, it is normal for one person to want sex more often than the other—this is typical. Physiologically, men and women are different, and this includes their individual sexual cycle. I have found it is very helpful for each spouse to understand their partner's cycle as well as their own. Just this one piece of information has turned attitudes around; I would even bet it has saved many relationships. There is power in knowing "what is normal." First off, it is typical for 70 to 80 percent of men to want or need sex more often than women. But there are about 20 to 30 percent of women who desire sexual activity more than their husbands. This is one piece of information worth knowing and accepting. Where do you and your spouse fall in connection with sexual desire? Who wants sexual intimacy more often?

Second, it is important to understand some basic, physiological differences between men and women. Typically, a woman's body is designed to be interested in sexual activity about once a month for a couple of days at the peak of her menstrual cycle. So if she bases her feelings for sex just on hormones, she only "feels" like having sex once a month. (I understand that love, sexual expression, and romance are more complex than just responding to the menstrual cycle, but this provides a baseline.)

On the other hand, the typical male has a completely different cycle sexually. He produces 100 million to 200 million "little Navy guys" (sperm) every day, and when his body builds up 400 million to 500 million sperm, it is time to launch the boats, if you will. This means that the average man is interested in sexual activity and release every other day to every five days. (Obviously, individual men can vary on this issue as psychological, physical, emotional, and spiritual factors can cause wide variance to this cycle.)

Most often, the man will be way more interested in sexual activity than his wife. Whatever the specific timing of you and your spouse's sexual build up and release cycle, it will be different for the man and the woman. It is very helpful for a couple to establish the sexual needs for each spouse and build the sexual schedule around the typical week and for special occasions.

If you wait until the mood is "right," both of you can regularly feel frustrated and rejected. Both spouses have sexual needs that have to be met, and the only way I have discovered to make this happen is by scheduling it regularly around the one with the stronger need. For 70 to 80 percent of the marriages, this will be around the man's need, and for the other 20 to 30 percent, it will be around the woman's need. Yes, there are marriages when both spouses are equally yoked in their constant desire, which is a wonderful blessing, but this is extremely rare.

What should the schedule look like? It depends. There are a few questions that need answering. I will ask these very matter-of-factly and it will hopefully open a dialogue on this topic with your spouse. This area cannot be left up to "when you feel like it." That kind of thinking will always leave the one least interested in charge of this area and one spouse incredibly frustrated. Let's start with these:

> *Who has the greater need, and how often does that spouse need sexual release?*
>
> *How many times per week and per month should you plan to have sex to meet the needs?*
>
> *What times of day are best: Are mornings better? Are evenings better?*

Are weekends better?

When are both people likely to be free from distractions or not too tired?

This entire concept is baffling to many couples in the early years of marriage. They enter marriage believing they will only have sex when both people feel like it. And in the beginning of the marriage, that can be quite often! But they find out sooner or later this only goes so far. What I have found is that couples who have a ridiculously great marriage schedule time for sexual activity every week to meet the sexual needs of the most sexually interested person in the relationship. Those who don't meet this need in a regular, planned way typically do not have a great marriage.

It is best to move beyond the romantic ideals that movies portray when it comes to physical, sexual expressions in marriage. It can't be based on feelings and desires alone. When a couple is dating, they always want to be with the other person, and they have all kinds of hormones firing, pushing them to want to express their love to the fullest as soon as possible. But it will not be like that all the time in the marriage.

I think it is also helpful to demystify some things about orgasms. Couples should stop chasing the mutual orgasm, which can happen but rarely does. Usually the best way to enjoy a satisfying sexual encounter with your spouse is to bring one person to climax and then the other. It is often best (but not always) for the more slowly-responding person to be brought to climax first and then focus on bringing the quick-responder to climax. This requires self-control by the quick-responding partner and will take time to master. One person is brought to climax, then the other. This is a very satisfying way to make sure that both people in the relationship fully enjoy intimacy.

I heard about one woman who felt very degraded and used by her husband because he never took the time to bring her to orgasm. His habit was to make sex all about him and meeting his own needs, which is wrong. Yes, there will be times when the focus should be on meeting the need of one spouse, but it should be voluntary and in the spirit of ministering to each other. Healthy sex is fulfilling and gratifying for both partners. Sex is not about taking but is an intimate act of giving to one's spouse and communicating with them.

Scheduling and planning intimacy may seem rigid or unromantic. Interestingly enough, the couples who schedule their times of intimacy usually are more satisfied with their sex life than couples who don't. That is because couples who schedule sex have stronger feelings for each other because they know they can count on their spouse to meet them where they are. It also bonds them together like nothing else can. And it communicates caring and compassion, love and sacrifice like no other action in marriage.

For the partner who is more interested in sexual intimacy than the other person, waiting for the disinterested person to actually get in the mood can set up all kinds of issues—feelings of insecurity, wandering eyes, guilt, and lustful tendencies. Your spouse doesn't want to feel that way and neither should you want them to feel that way. It is easier on both partners if sexual activity is planned and regular. Schedule the time for sexual expression just as you would plan to meet the eating need, the talking need, and the relaxing need. It brings predictability and security to this very personal area.

There are other things to consider when scheduling intimacy. You need to understand the various ways both people find sexual expression appropriate. Every couple has circumstances and life stages that are different, and they will need to adapt the schedule accordingly.

Generally, there are three different types of sexual expression in marriage: Wow! sex, normal sex, quickie sex. Different couples call these expressions by different names, but great couples all know about these different ways of enjoying one another. In strained marriages, I find that one or both of the spouses does not believe they are having real sex if it is not an eleven on a ten scale. That is not realistic or fair. Not every meal you eat will be amazing. Not every sleep will be fantastic. Not every movie or television program you watch will be the best ever. Neither will every sexual encounter be soul-stirring and life-altering. God has given us sexual expression for procreation, pleasure, and bonding. As one woman stated to me regarding the sexual expression in her own marriage, "Sometimes the tide is in, and sometimes the tide is out." This is a much more realistic description for how it really is.

Let me describe the three different expressions in a little more detail, and you can think about how and when these would be placed within your weekly schedule.

Wow! Sex

This is where both people are interested and committed to intimacy. This involves talking, sharing, caressing, undressing, foreplay, and intercourse. It is usually best for one partner to bring the slower-responding partner (usually the woman) to climax before the faster-responding person is brought to climax. Usually, a man who climaxes first becomes disinterested in sexual activity quickly after, but the woman will usually continue to be interested in sexual intimacy and closeness long after her climax. This is why often it is best to bring her to climax first before moving to satisfy her husband. On average, Wow! sex takes place once or maybe a few times per month. This is the kind of sex that brings about the most amount of bonding and intimacy between the partners.

NORMAL SEX

In this expression of sex, one person is highly interested and the other person is not excited and potentially emotionally reluctant, but can be brought into the experience if treated well beforehand. The love in the relationship usually determines how often the reluctant one is willing to move into this type of sexual intimacy. This level of sexual expression is typically a once-a-week occurrence in America at present. In this form of sex, both people are fully engaged, both naked, and both participating and coming to climax. This is true even though one of the partners started out being reluctant or not interested.

QUICKIE SEX

This type of sexual expression happens when the person with the greater need for sexual intimacy is brought to climax without their spouse engaging sexually or even seeking climax. He or she demonstrates a willingness to minister to the needs of the more interested or needy spouse until they experience sexual release or climax. This is a selfless action for the good of the other spouse and marriage. This might be something that needs to happen two to three times per week depending on how often the more interested spouse needs it (per their sexual cycle).

Within the timeframe of a month, couples should engage in all three of these sexual expressions. A couple with a healthy sex life will make sure they do. The health and frequency of their sex life will help create the ridiculously great marriage they are wanting. These times can be scheduled and planned for just like anything else. Here are some guidelines for each of these:

SEXUAL EXPRESSION GUIDELINES

Expression	WOW!	Normal	Quickie
Duration	2 - 3 Hours	20 minutes to 1 hour	5 - 10 minutes
Frequency	1 - 4 times per month	1 - 2 times per week	1 - 2 times per week

Let me quote Pastor Jud Boise from his excellent upcoming book, *What's for Dessert?*:

> Our bodies were designed to be awake for a certain number of hours and then sleep, eat on a regular basis, exercise on a regular basis, and I would say, it works best when we have sex on a regular basis. So, what is regular? For food, we eat three times a day. Sorry guys, I'm not recommending that we have sex three times a day. Similarly, we wouldn't exercise three times a day. Sex varies per couple. For some couples, five times a week is their normal; for others, once every other week is their normal. But there is regularity. It varies widely per couple. The important thing is to discuss how often you want to eat (have sex) and set a schedule. If you don't plan it, it won't happen. If you don't calendar it, it may not happen. Time flies by. So, my recommendation is to first set a schedule and try it for a month. At the end of the month, discuss how it went.[1]

Let's look at an example of planning out sexual activity for a typical week that would meet the needs of both people. The following is just a possible scenario for sexual activity for a typical husband and wife who have a few young kids and a date on Friday nights.

SAMPLE INTIMACY SCHEDULE

Week #	Sunday	Monday	Tuesday	Wednesday	Thursday	Friday	Saturday
1.	After church, during kids naps. (Normal) 30 mins			Before the kids get up and the day gets started. (Quickie) 15 mins		After our date before midnight. (Normal) 15-45 mins	
2.	After Sunday nap. (WOW! or Normal) up to 1 hour				When kids are in bed. (Quickie) 15 minutes		
3.		Before the week gets started. (Quickie) 10 mins		While the kids are doing homework. (Quickie) 15 mins			After the kids go to bed. (Normal) 15 - 45 mins
4.			After the kids go to bed. (Normal) 15-30 mins			After date night. (WOW!) 3 hours with foreplay and talking	

This sample schedule is only designed to get you talking as a couple about where and when each of you would put the various needed sexual encounters. Of course, it will look differently if you don't have children, but in general, you will want to consider things like schedules, work commitments, energy levels, menstrual cycles, travel, and date nights. With your spouse, plan your intimacy time for the week and/or month. Determine how much time you can take and which type of sexual expression you will plan for. Remember to take time for talking, foreplay, and intercourse. I think this is a great way to approach this idea of scheduling intimacy. If both husband and wife know what is coming and about how long it will take, it allows for great connection and encouragement. Go ahead and plan out the week or month ahead.

The area of sexual intimacy can be a very difficult for some couples for a variety of reasons. If you feel you need more help, consider checking out a few resources, including *Intended for Pleasure* by Ed and Gaye Wheat, *The Act of Marriage* by Tim and Beverly LaHaye, and *What's for Dessert?* by Jud and Mary Boise (coming in 2020). I would also recommend seeing a trusted Christian counselor for additional help.

One of the most wonderful benefits of marriage is sexual expression. Sex is wonderful and can help build a lasting relationship. When a husband and a wife are serving and being served in transparency and honesty, the relationship blossoms. Both parties need to be loved sexually and to give love sexually. The promise of sex should not be held captive by the emotions of one spouse. We don't think anything is wrong with scheduling meals, shower times, dates, and work. So too we should schedule sexual expression with one another and learn how to express and receive love from our spouse in those times. You and your spouse will share in the gift of sex thousands of times in your marriage. It is so helpful to know when it's coming; of course, spontaneity is wonderful too.

I hope this chapter on the details and various expressions of sexual activities in marriage will help you as a couple to build a ridiculously great marriage. It is things like this—scheduling time for sexual intimacy—that helps to accomplish this.

Habit #9

Eat One Meal Together Every Day

One of the things that is destroying lots of marriages is workaholism or overworking. Men and women are working constantly and either do not take time or have time to be with their spouse or their families. But couples in great marriages make time to be together, usually around a meal.

Before Dana and I got married, I was used to working about a hundred hours a week. There was always something to do. I found when I was single that if I visited a family's house at breakfast, lunch, or dinner, I did not have to make dinner, eat alone, or pay for the meal! Plus, it was great for connection to the congregation. It was a win for me all the way around as a single pastor. After Dana and I married, you can imagine this did not last long. My wife did not want to be dragged around from one house to another with no private time to ourselves. We needed to have our own breakfasts, our own lunches, and our own dinners together. A few times a week, we missed eating together because of the press of the schedule but not all the time.

This little habit was all her doing and has been huge for us as we have sought to develop a ridiculously delightful marriage and emotionally stable, healthy kids. Interestingly enough, eating meals together as a family is cited by Columbia University as a key ingredient to "drug proof" kids.[1]

There is something special about eating with other people. Sharing meal times strengthens bonds with the people we really care about, those we should care about, or those we ought to get to know. The individual deliberate attention given over a meal communicates love and grace like no other way. Just eating with another person even if you don't do much talking allows for warmth, connection, and joy. Unfortunately, our culture today is made up of people who are so sped up or plugged in they don't have time to do the crucial habits needed to maintain a healthy relationship, like have a simple meal together.

In our family, we have a few ground rules that help our meals become rich, meaningful times of connection and reflection for everyone involved. I would like to share a few of these with you now.

GROUND RULE 1: ONE-MEAL-A-DAY MINIMUM

Couples and families ought to commit to eating at least one meal together each day. That's what we do in our family. We have had to be creative at times, but we take it very seriously. Great couples take this habit seriously and work hard to protect it, just as we have. If you are going through a period where you or one of the family members is especially busy, make sure the one-meal minimum is still met. It could be the evening, mid-day, or the morning meal. I know one man who realized the demands on his time just kept growing, so he blocked out all meal times to be with his family. He was available for all the people who wanted him at the other times of the day, but every meal time he was with his family. In this way, he spent three-plus hours with his family every day. This is an extreme example of a person who saw the value of eating with his family—he made it work for him even though he was busy. Don't miss the value of eating with your spouse and family. The benefits are more than you think they would be.

Talk with your spouse about which meal is best to set aside to have together as a couple and as a family. It will usually be the same time each day, but on the weekends or special work days, it may be a different time. This is especially true when there are elementary school-aged children at home and they begin to have practices scheduled during the dinner times. But in those cases, maybe breakfast is the best time to eat together or a snack after practice.[2] The point is that we ought to work hard at preserving a meal time together—a sacred time for coming together to share the day's events, each other, and more.

GROUND RULE 2: ELIMINATE DISTRACTIONS, NON-NEGOTIABLE

Distractions are everywhere these days, pulling at us in one direction or another. TVs, cell phones, and personal electronic devices are our nemeses when it comes to focused meal times. These outside distractions take us away from the people before us in the here and now and transport us into another place with another group of people who have nothing to do with our lives and maybe aren't even real! Yes, I know there is interesting information on your phone or your book or your TV that you would rather look at, but constantly doing so will cut you off from the people who need to be a part of your life.

Recently, a family of six was out at a restaurant having dinner, and I noticed every single one of the kids were plugged into their own separate devices. Some were playing video games and others were watching a movie. My first thought was that it was a strategic way for the mom and dad to have some time to talk together, which would have made some sense except they were sitting clear on the opposite side of the table with the children between them. It seemed like a very lonely situation for all of them. Sadly, I see more and more of this everywhere I go.

Husbands and wives, especially, need to take advantage of their designated meal time together. We're all so busy these days and time together is precious with all we have going on. Date night should be held in high esteem, reserved only for the two of you without children. But how often have I seen a man and a woman on what seems like a date, where one or both people are on their phones. So sad! I see it all the time in restaurants near where I live, and I'm sure you do too. Relationships do not thrive when outside distractions are the focus. We need to put down our cell phones and talk to each other and really listen.

I would highly recommend implementing a non-negotiable, no-electronics-at-the-table rule for your family. This may seem harsh, but you would be surprised how easy it is for this little ritual to slip away. Before we know it, we are eating by ourselves watching little screens or big ones, and missing out on the crucial little pieces that keep a relationship together. We are able to learn so many little things about each other if we just turn off our devices during the meal. That little screen will always seem more interesting, but it really isn't.

One restaurant I heard about has a bag located next to their dining tables for patrons to place their devices to facilitate conversation and togetherness. These folks realize this meal time might be the only chance families and friends have focused attention on each other that day, and they don't want them to miss out on that opportunity. They have the right idea. I wish all restaurants did that! Eating a meal together every day is worth fighting for. (Exceptions would be if you are a doctor on-call or expecting a very important phone call.)

GROUND RULE 3: ASK QUESTIONS ABOUT EVERYONE AND EVERYTHING

Maybe you already eat together on a regular basis, and perhaps you even have a no-electronics rule in place. What else can you do to maximize these precious times together? What can you talk about to keep it fresh and interesting? Meal times are really just about being together, but great dialogue takes this time to a whole new level.

Become lovingly curious about everything in your spouse's life. Ask questions because you really want to learn. Ask them about what they're are thinking about. Ask them how they feel about some news item. Ask them about three fun things they would like to do. My family has learned that curiosity is the key to meaty conversations and deeper connection. Becoming curious about everyone and everything is hugely rewarding, even if you have no personal interest in that area. There is so much to talk about besides the day's events.

I have found that my world is expanded so powerfully when I can get people talking about the things they notice and the things they are passionate about or the struggles they are going through. Isn't this the whole point of the family meal or a husband and a wife eating together—to get to know one another better, to connect? Develop a curiosity about the other person's life. Find out how they tick. If you do, I think you will find life will get much more interesting for you.

Being curious means asking questions to get to know them, not interrogating the other person or making judgments about what they're saying. I want to suggest three different types of questions to explore. Don't feel like you need to follow these exactly, but these areas can be helpful to launch your conversations. The main thing is to be curious and ask questions—about their experiences, their relationships, and how they are doing spiritually. Let me warn you that much of the information you will receive in answer to your questions will be of no immediate, practical use in your life, except to say to the other person that you love them because you are listening to them intentionally. Here are a number of things to talk about to have a wonderful, growth-oriented meal time together.

THREE TYPES OF QUESTIONS TO EXPLORE DURING MEALTIME

1. Experiential Questions

These are the kinds of questions that give the person a chance to tell you about themselves in some ordered fashion. You don't go after the most juicy or difficult topic right off the bat; you let them unwind who they are in a more meandering fashion. One sample question could be, "Tell me about your day from beginning to end."

This is such a great question to glean all the interesting, funny, significant, or even disturbing things that happened to the other person during the day. For instance, I know that my wife's work day consists of waking up, the morning rituals, commuting to work, getting started that day, seeing patients, charting on each patient, taking a lunch and talking to her colleagues, seeing more patients, trying to catch up with her phone messages, charts, approvals from the insurance companies, end-of-the-day collegial interactions, the return commute, and finally arrival at home. But lots of interesting, emotional, difficult, developmental, and funny things could have happened in any of those sections. I want to know about all of it! I ask about the various areas to see if something happened that she would normally pass over—a highlight or a low light of that day.

Ask about the various areas to see if something happened that she would normally pass over—a highlight or a low light of that day. Ask about your spouse's day and listen to what they found interesting and fascinating about it. If my wife starts talking in detail about any of these areas, then I will ask at least two more questions about what she went through.

Another good question is, "Did you read or hear anything today that was funny, troubling, alarming, or encouraging?" I like this question because it will sometimes uncover something that does not come out in other types of conversation. Maybe my wife listened to an audible book or read something in a devotional that is really profound or interesting. It is also good to see what strikes your spouse or family members as funny. Their sense of humor may not be yours, but you get a window into their soul when they share.

How about this question, "Tell me something about your elementary (middle, high) school years that I don't know?" This type of question may bring up something like a time in high school or college when something happened that was significant to them. I asked this question to my wife the other day and it was wonderful—hearing all the memories she had flooding into her memory. Then she turned the question around and asked me about my elementary years, and I talked with her about friends from those years who she had never heard about.

You can get some very interesting dialogue going with this type of question: "What is your earliest memory of money?" I am amazed at the power of this question. So often our attitudes toward money are formed around our first memories of money being money. If our attitudes are formed out of a misperception of money, then we may limp through life with an inaccurate attitude toward money. This can be a very interesting and helpful question to all of the members of your family. Here are some more examples of other questions that can really spark good conversation to uncover experiences:

Are there any jobs you have had that I don't know about?

Tell me about three jobs you would never want to do and why?

Who are three friends you have had who I probably don't know about?

Who would you say have been your three most significant enemies in your life and why?

If you could change three problems in society what would they be?

What are five of your accomplishments, achievements, or significant events I might not know about?

What were three things you remember feeling as a youngster?

What were your dreams when you were in elementary school, middle school, and/or high school?

When would you say you were closest to God and why?

What are the three to five most meaningful Scripture verses to you and why?

2. **Relationship Questions**

These are the type of questions you can ask the other person about the ten major relationships of life (God, self, spouse, family, work/school, finances, church, friends, community, enemies). This really is very enjoyable and profitable for all parties, because the more we show interest in other people, the more they show interest in us. To know which of the ten relationships to start with, throw out some leading questions to see which of the relationships the other person wants to talk about. If they are animated by the question, you'll know you've hit on something they want to share more about, then extend the questions from there. Here are some examples:

Is anything interesting or challenging coming up at work or school?

Are you saving up for anything exciting or necessary?

Do you have any dream trips or vacations planned?

What are you the most excited about learning?

What changes are planned at work that excite you?

What do you find yourself thinking about family?

How was your quiet time with God, or how is your spiritual life going?

Are you planning anything interesting with your friends?

What is happening at your church?

Is anything happening in the community that interests you?

Is anyone bothering you lately?

There are additional questions for each relationship located in appendix 1.

3. **Spiritual Development Questions**

   Another great exercise is to turn a portion of the meal you spend together into a spiritual sharing time by talking about what God is teaching each of you and how you are interacting with Him in the problems of the day. When a couple or family brings God into their meal times, it makes sure that spirituality is a part of how they live their everyday life. Begin by praying at the start of the meal, then read a devotional thought or a Scripture during some portion of the meal. Ask questions about what God is saying to them. When you read a passage of Scripture out loud at dinner, you can ask for comments on what the other person thinks it means and how it could be applied. This will spark an interesting discussion.

PRACTICAL MEAL-TIME HABITS

This is a habit that makes a marriage ridiculously great. Eating at least one meal together is a high priority in a great couple's day. You're armed with examples of types of questions you can ask to really dig deep. Now all that's needed is the habit itself! Here are some steps to make eating together a habit.

1. Incorporate meal times together into the weekly planning meeting you have with your spouse (see habit #2). Put it on the calendar just like you would any appointment, event, or obligation. Do everything you can to protect the designated time.

2. Be creative about when to have this meal time together. Choose breakfast, lunch, dinner, or a break time—whichever time gives you the best chance to talk and connect as a couple and as a family.

3. Communicate when this meal time will be with all family members so everyone is on the same page about where they need to be at these times. Set the expectation to participate early on.

4. If eating together is new to you, start with one meal per week and increase from there. If you miss a meal, pick it up at the next opportunity. The goal is to eat together a minimum of one time every day.

5. Instigate a non-negotiable, no-electronics-at-meal-time rule, unless you're a doctor on-call or you're expecting a critical phone call.

6. Remember the purpose—to connect and get to know one another at deeper levels. The more you eat together, the better. Ask questions, lean in, and listen. The results will be ridiculous.

Make Decisions Together

How do you come to agreement when you and your spouse don't agree? Many couples have either a pattern of fighting or they just give in, both of which are not helpful. One of the great values in every great marriage is trust. Building up trust is essential in a marriage. Working through difficulties and disagreements can either build trust or destroy it. The system I am suggesting in this chapter is not as easy as "my wife decides everything" or "my husband makes all the decisions," but it does build huge amounts of trust. Building trust is relational wealth.

In marriage, you can expect disagreements over all kinds of things that involve making decisions. These involve things like what to spend your tax return on, remodeling the house, where to move, what kind of car to purchase, what to do on vacation, what the budget amounts are for weekly spending, how to handle the relatives, parenting decisions, what food to eat, and so on. Of course, there will be a number of things you disagree about that don't require a decision, like favorite colors or sports teams, favorite foods, clothing styles, or music. These don't necessarily impact the other person, though I suppose it can when each spouse supports rival sports teams! Couples who have a ridiculously great marriage put some sort of system in place to come to agreement. This habit is a game-changer if you use it wisely.

In this chapter, I will talk about how to develop a decision-making system that works. My wife and I faced a decision just the other day about exercise: where to exercise, how to exercise, how much to spend, would we do it together or separately. We both had definite ideas and opinions. Instead of fighting about it or jockeying for our own way, we put our "dilemma" through our system and came up with a much better decision than either of us would have had on our own. It took us a month to put all the options, ideas, and perspectives through our system to come out with something that both of us wholeheartedly support. In the grand scheme of things, it is not a huge decision, but the way we came to agreement, and the way we both support the decision, strengthens our marriage rather than weakens it.

And this is the point of this habit. There needs to be a system in place in your marriage to help you make decisions together as a couple. I think you'll see that this one habit can help you avoid a lot of grief and stress throughout your years together.

THE BENEFITS OF DECIDING THINGS TOGETHER

Great couples find a way to work through decisions together. You are a team. If a marriage is going to be a winning team, the players have to agree on the plays. You both have to be moving forward in the same direction to achieve the desired result. An inability to decide things together in marriage not only destroys trust and love, but it distracts and diverts attention away from what is really important—the relationship itself. Remember, the win is when you, your spouse, and God all win (the triple-win approach that I talked about in habit #6).

Having a system in place before a disagreement even comes up is ideal but not always possible. There should be a safe place to share each of your own opinions, preferences, and desires to find wisdom over issues together. Too often I watch couples fight, spend, scream, cry, ignore, seethe, hate, and selfishly cling to their own ideas, which creates so much hurt and rifts in the relationship. Usually, it is because there is no system in place to talk through ideas, but the breakdown also happens because of personality differences and blaming.

For many of the couples I counsel, I have found there to be one spouse with a stronger more dominant personality, and one with a weaker, more compliant or peacemaking personality. Friction builds up when the spouse with the dominant personality bulldozes over the spouse with the weaker personality. So what needs to happen is for the spouse with the stronger, louder personality to draw out the quieter one and learn how to blend their spouse's needs and desires with their own. When they can do this, the results are wonderful.

Blaming is a huge problem in unhealthy marriages. This process helps you eliminate blame toward your spouse for decisions that didn't go well. I have watched many couples fumble in this area. One spouse gives in to the decision of the other spouse, almost with the idea that if this doesn't work, they can hold it over their head for the rest of their life.

This whole system helps you find the wise decision together. The two of you work through the process of finding wisdom until it has been found, and then implement the wise decision you have found *together*. If a decision doesn't go as planned, there is no need to blame! It was a decision made by *both* of you. You helped make the decision, and both of you will be needed to help rescue or move on from the decision. Simply go back to the process and put the new situation and your needed response into the processes.

If you are going to have a ridiculously great marriage, then you must have a process in place to move you past only your point of view. God put you two people together for a reason—to prosper and glorify Him. Only when both people's wisdom and perspectives are voiced and considered will this happen. This process can take five minutes or it can take much longer to arrive at a wise decision, but it is totally worth it. Let me introduce this process now.

FIVE-STEP DECISION-MAKING PROCESS

My wife and I use this process all the time to make many different kinds of decisions. I have also personally witnessed how this system can be incredibly helpful at pushing couples toward wisdom and unity. It can be used for any dispute no matter how large or small. Just plug in the different perspectives, go through the phases, and out will come a wiser perspective than when you started. A little humility is required at the start, because it means you are willing to admit you do not have all knowledge or all options at the beginning. And it means you value your spouse more than the outcome of the decision itself. If you look back at habit #6, "Seek Wisdom, Not Your Own Way," wisdom means finding what is best for everyone—something both of you can support.

This decision-making process has five phases: a way to hear different opinions, collect facts, talk to wise people, pray, and then come to a mutual decision. You are trying to arrive at a place of wisdom where God wins, the other person wins, and you win. This could take considerably more time to arrive at a decision than what you're used to, but allow for it; the wiser decision is the winning decision. Here are the five phases for making a wise decision together.

Phase One: Discuss Perspectives

This phase is reserved for giving opinions, perspectives, and desires. *Both* people get to talk, first one, then the other. Whatever the issue is, talk about what each of you would like to see happen. What do you want to do with the money, time, energy, children, and why? No decisions are to be made here or immediately following. This is just an in-take phase. We are just listening to each other. Suspend your judgment of whether what they are saying is a good idea or a bad idea.

Listen to what is being said and make sure you hear their idea and perspective. This is not the time to point out the weakness in what they are saying; critique will come later. Both people get to ask questions about the other person's perspective, but not to run it down. The goal is to understand what the other person is saying. This is also not to be an argument but a chance to hear another perspective. If you listen well, then you can decide well. Many times, couples find that a little bit of both people's perspective can be used to make a better decision in the end. I like to say, "There are always options." "Let me know what you think."

I have heard about some couples who put a card on the table to remind them that this part is just a discussion—no decisions can come out of this phase of the process. It's interesting because I've learned that some people don't want to listen to their spouse's ideas for fear it suggests they are in favor of it! But this isn't true nor is it fair. Make it clear that this is a time for hearing what the other person is saying, not arguing for your position or deciding anything.

This phase is like a brainstorming session in which everyone gets their ideas out on the table. Listening to each other does not mean agreement. Letting both people give ideas and solutions is a way of loving each other. We all want to feel listened to and understood. Our ideas may prove to need amending or discarding later but right now we are just listening to each other. Just because there is listening doesn't mean it will be done your way; it is only communicating options. Once each person has had a chance to put their perspective on the table, it's time to move on to phase two.

Phase 2: Explore Options

In this phase, it is time to explore the various options that have been suggested. This could combine both people's perspectives or other ideas that come to mind now that everything is on the table. You are not trying to prove one person right and another person wrong. You are trying to find wisdom where everyone wins and God is pleased. Wisdom is the goal and it usually is some combination of ideas. What are all the options we have for using this time, changing our children's mind, spending this money, and so forth? You can't pick the best option until you know what they are.

You are searching for options and will continue to look for wise options throughout this decision-making process. When you are in the options phase, you are hopeful you and your spouse will come across other options neither of you had thought of before. Begin by discussing the various options. What ideas do each of you have to accomplish this? How would you rate each option? Are they viable? Do they achieve what you're trying to do? If not, then you need more information, which phase three will accomplish.

Phase 3: Seek Outside Counsel

At this point, you begin to actively search for new wisdom and options through other people, books, magazines, or websites to help you make a wise decision. Who do we need to talk to? Who can give us the best wisdom? One time, I asked Dana who she wanted me to talk to about a purchase we were looking at making, and she said her dad and the consumer's reports website. Both of these options have been very helpful over the years as we have worked through the various decisions we needed to make.

For us, this phase can last a few hours or even a few years at times. If we have a very difficult decision to make, such as changing jobs or having another child, this counsel phase can take a long time. It is always helpful to have lots of wise people to get advice from. Your sources of wisdom should be broad enough not to just convince you that you were right in the first place. Talk to *thoughtful* people. Talk to *successful* people. Don't get advice from the people who have failed every time at the thing they are advising you on!

Look for trustworthy sources who can give you additional perspectives and ways of doing things. These are people who will ask you good questions and want to see you succeed. Hopefully, some options will begin to fade out, while others become more highlighted, or new options will come to the surface you hadn't considered before. This is the goal of phase three. Once you have some good, viable options in front of you, now it's time for phase four—pray about them.

Phase 4: Prayer

This phase is critical for determining wisdom in a decision. I strongly suggest that both of you take the time to pray individually and spend some time praying together about the decision. Honestly kneel before God and let Him know, in the presence of the other person, that you want wisdom not just your way. Ask God for His wisdom and His guidance. He will guide those who really want His direction—He has told us He will (Jas. 1:5).

We have an ottoman our family gathers around and uses to focus our times of prayer together. We will actually say, "It is time to take this to the prayer ottoman." And then we will kneel and pray bringing up our various ideas, points of view, and desire for God's wisdom on the issue. Wherever you decide to pray, pray about the decision together and see how God directs you. Both people pray. Both people plead with God for wisdom not their way. My wife and I pay special attention to the ideas, people, articles, and insights that come to us in the hours and days after we have prayed around the ottoman about a decision we are facing.

This is not a perfunctory exercise, but a real seeking of wisdom through prayer, Scripture, promptings of the Holy Spirit, individuals, circumstances, and so on. Sometimes couples pray in ways that suggests they don't expect anything to happen when they pray. This is not that type of prayer. This type of prayer expects God to give you wisdom, as James 1:5 says, "If any of you lacks wisdom, let him ask God, who gives to all without reproach, and it will be given to him." Pray and expect God to answer. Once you have prayed, it is almost decision time.

Phase 5: Make the Decision

Making the decision is also a phase. I do not believe that impulse decisions are wise decisions. Impulsive decisions can destroy relationships. Make sure that everyone is on the same page. Always build into the decision process a feedback or checkback system, "Are we agreed that this is the decision that is best or wisest in this situation?" Here is how I have seen it work best. When the combined wisdom seems clear, the husband should say something like, "It seems like we agree that _____ is our decision. Do you agree? If you have new wisdom or information, let's look at it now."

Everyone must be open to new information or new concerns or new insights as these can lead to an even better decision. Stating the potential decision before it is made clarifies the decision and also gives the other spouse a chance to speak up and agree with it, disagree with it, or clarify it in their own words. If your partner doesn't agree that this decision is the obvious wise choice, or it isn't what they thought it was, then it is time to start the process all over again for these new ideas, options, and directions.

I can't stress enough about not hurrying through this process. Don't be in a big hurry...focus on finding wisdom. The Proverbs say repeatedly that wisdom must be sought for like silver and pursued like gold (Prov. 3:13–15). The choices that allow everyone to win are not always obvious and need to be hunted down (Prov. 2:2–6). I have watched couples start over several times as they moved together toward the wise decision that they could both live with. Great couples work together—they don't necessarily make the perfect decision every time, but they try to. It is the process of talking, listening, checking with others, finding places of compromise, looking for new ideas, researching, growing your ideas, praying together, and deciding *together* that strengthens the marriage.

There is a time for a decision to be made, and some come quickly and some allow much more time. The goal is wisdom which requires going beyond your own ideas. Don't let it throw you off that one spouse makes decisions slower and one wants to make decisions faster. There can be a danger of delaying a decision so long that the decision is made for you. I have found that if you aim for wisdom, there is always enough time to find it. You are fighting two impulses: making an impulsive or selfish choice, and making no decision at all because you can't talk about your differing points of view.

Seek wisdom and you will find it. Of course, you may adapt and adjust this system to suit the type of decision you are trying to make as a couple. But find a way to involve both people in the process without one person's selfish perspectives dominating the way the marriage functions. Don't fight... find wisdom. Almost everyone can agree that what is needed is wisdom, so going after wisdom unifies the relationship. There are always options if both spouses will be reasonable.

What are some decisions you and your spouse could take through this five-step decision-making process? Think if there are any areas of contention or disagreement that are causing stress to the relationship, and start with the biggest one first. Write them down here.

1.

2.

3.

ESTABLISH PRESET DECISIONS

Every marriage needs to also have preset decisions for certain things. Life is way simpler if you have regular routines that flow out of preset decisions. These decisions will likely need to be revisited as the kids get older or as work changes or if something else changes in life that impacts one of the routines. That's normal and to be expected.

Many people bring the preset decisions of their own families into their marriage and these need to be discussed by the couple, because the two different families' preset decisions may be different than what either of you want. You will need to run these differences through the five-phase process and come to a wise decision for your own marriage on these things. One example could be who does which chores. Or how will we spend our weekends? There is not a right or wrong way as long as you both agree on what to do for the good of your own family.

In the early months of our marriage, we discovered the need to have some preset decisions around our finances after I had bought something that cost $150 without checking with Dana. We decided we needed a rule about how much we could spend without having to check with the other person. Our first decision was that it needed to be $20. As our marriage has gone along, we have revisited that decision and raised it to $100 because we now know so much more about each other and what would type of purchases trouble our spouse.

In our household, Dana and I decided together that I am really bad with trying to fix things around the house. I usually mess things up and get frustrated in the process. So after much discussion, options, and counsel, as well as prayer and preliminary decisions, we have a list of highly recommended home repair people who Dana can call to fix things around the house for less than $100 dollars in any given month. She lets me know she is doing this so the budget works, and I'm happy to let her do this.

Another preset decision we made later revolved around our children and sleepovers. We decided, after much discussion, that to keep our kids safe, we would allow them to have sleepovers after they were ten years of age. That is not what every family does, but it worked for our family. I can also remember we had preset decisions each week for the girls as to what we would work on to train that particular child that week, as well as the positive and negative training techniques for that child. We posted the focus and training techniques in prominent places around the house for the week to remind us.

For my work, we went through many discussions and much counsel and prayer in regards to how many nights I could be out each week to maintain church ministry and our family. Together we decided I could be at church three nights a week and should be home four nights a week in order to let our children and my wife know they were more important than my job. I could do a little work on the computer, but I was to be available to them for homework, playing, dates, talking, and so forth. There are hundreds of these types of decisions that you can make ahead of time together, which can function for a week, a month, a year, or beyond.

What are some decisions you can set up ahead of time for you, your spouse, or your family? List some of your ideas here, or write down any you have already put in place.

1.

2.

3.

4.

5.

Let me say that making decisions together does not have to be hard. There is great strength to giving the person who is in charge of doing a task, or who has greater expertise in an area, the greater weight in the decision-making process. I can remember when Dana and I tried to decide about which vacuum cleaner we were going to buy. My wife wanted an upright one, and I was sold on the wonder of the horizontal cannister. We went through the whole process I outlined above. We found that both are good and clean about the same; but in the end, it came down to who would actually be vacuuming more. Since she would be the one operating the vacuum much more than me, we went with her wisdom and choice.

The point of this habit is to build trust and unity in the marriage. God put you together to make decisions together, not just one of you. Your decisions will be different from the decisions that other couples make, but if made together in unity, you own them together whatever the outcome. It will make your marriage stronger because you both were involved in the decision.

Every couple needs a system to bring their concerns, ideas, and disagreements to, so that a great decision or change can be made to improve the marriage. If there is no system in place, then the couple is stuck with the level of wisdom of only one of the partners, instead of both partners and God's. If both people realize there is a way to talk about the things they might see differently than their spouse, then there is great hope in the marriage for both partners. You may not use this system, but you need some kind of system to talk things over and make decisions. Try this method and find ways to improve it. Make it work for you.

Learn to Forgive or
Live in a Toxic Relationship

N o one knowingly sits in a vat of toxic lye. The moment we realize we had just sat down in a toxic stew, we would get up immediately. Unfortunately, many couples are in a poisonous vat of emotions and hurts, hoping their marriage will survive. This is no way to live, and it certainly isn't what God intended for our marriages. That is why we must eliminate all toxins, poisons, and corrosive emotions that destroy marriages. This removing ourselves from toxic emotions is the crux of this next essential habit—*Learn to Forgive or Live in a Toxic Relationship.* This habit, along with habit #2 on apologizing, is critical for a marriage to thrive.

Couples with a ridiculously great marriage have a clear and simple way of dealing with resentments, anger, hatred, and wounds about each other. This applies to both people, and both need to constantly do this. Each of you will be tempted to hold things against your spouse for the ways they inflict hurt whether on purpose or inadvertently. You may even feel justified for feeling this way, but I want to give you a word of caution: holding onto these emotions longterm is toxic and extremely dangerous. You must find a way to let these resentments go. We don't want to stuff them down, and we don't want to pretend they don't exist; instead, we must process them, neutralize them, and release them.

A word of balance is also needed here. If your resentments and toxic emotions are coming from legitimate physical, sexual, emotional abuse, you may need to look at stepping away from the relationship until those issues are addressed before you and the relationship can be healed. There are times when a temporary separation is warranted.

This may come as a news flash but neither you nor your spouse is perfect. You cannot expect them to be perfect any more than you want them to expect you to be perfect. Grace is needed all around to make a marriage work. They will do many things you wish they did not do, and they will fail to do many things you will wish they would do. You will have to learn to let these deficiencies go. You will have to learn to forgive them. On some of the issues, you may have to tell them how or why their actions or inactions hurt you; even then, you will need to let their slight, hurt, or wound go. In 1 Corinthians, Paul reminds us of the qualities of true, abiding love:

Love is patient, love is kind and is not jealous; love does not brag and is not arrogant, does not act unbecomingly; it does not seek its own, is not provoked, does not take into account a wrong suffered, does not rejoice in unrighteousness, but rejoices with the truth; bears all things, believes all things, hopes all things, endures all things. (1 Cor. 13:4–7)

I once counseled a woman who was very angry at her husband—both for a number of things he did and a whole host of things he did not do. She said she wouldn't divorce him, even though she really wanted to. Instead, she would take a different strategy—to not be around much. Her plan was to get involved in business, charity, church, and other functions and live a separate life from her husband. I talked with her for a long time about all of this, and I suggested a different strategy than the physical-distance strategy she wanted to implement. My strategy was for her to begin to forgive her husband for all the things she was holding against him. She was comparing him to an ideal husband, which no man could live up to. This perfect husband doesn't even exist anywhere. She was asking her husband to be what he could never be.

In her case, she was an extremely gifted leader, and she wanted him to be a better leader than her. She wanted him to take charge and lead the way on many things in the marriage. But he wasn't a born leader like her. I pointed out that this difference was one reason for their attraction—they complemented each other: her strength in leadership complemented his willingness to follow and adapt.

I wasn't sure if she would do it, but then a wonderful thing happened. This once-angry, on-her-way-to-bitterness wife took forgiving her husband seriously. She recounted how she went back in her memory and dug up every seed of bitterness about him she had planted. Some bitter roots had even grown into huge trees of resentment. It took some work, but their marriage has healed and they are doing extremely well. This couple went through many ups and downs for sure. But if there was no willingness to forgive, resentments *would* grow again and doom the marriage. It would have ended in divorce, and the physical distance or devastating emotional distance would have been profound.

How your marriage turns out is on you in this area of forgiveness. Forgiveness is a choice. Even though it can be hard, it is one of those things we must commit to. Great couples have to create a system where both people can let go of resentments to move forward with the relationship. Ultimately, the relationship is more important than your resentments, so let go of them and move the relationship forward. Let me add that if your spouse is physically, sexually, or mentally abusing you, please take the appropriate action to protect yourself and your children. Get professional help. But recognize even then you will have to process the pain and learn to forgive your spouse, so you can move on with your life.

One of the reasons this habit is so important is because of how easy it is to allow resentments about our spouse build up until they have choked out any love for them. The Scriptures are clear that we were not designed to handle bitterness, "Let all bitterness and wrath and anger and clamor and slander be put away from you, along with all malice" (Eph. 4:31), and "Pursue peace with all men, and the sanctification without which no one will see the Lord. See to it that no one comes short of the grace of God; that no root of bitterness springing up causes trouble, and by it many be defiled" (Heb. 12:14–15).

Bitterness is a toxin that twists and distorts our thinking; it damages us, affects others, and ruins our relationships. In the Lord's Prayer, Jesus alludes to this powerful place which forgiveness occupies. If you do not forgive those who trespass (or sin) against you, your heavenly Father will not forgive you either (Matt. 6:12, 14–15). Learn the freedom of forgiveness, and partner with God to build a great life.

FORGIVENESS IS LEARNED

In marriage, the relationship can only be sustained and enjoyable when both people are willing to overlook and forgive. Forgiveness is about so much more than a marriage relationship, but it can be focused in that relationship as the hurts pile up over time. In this section, I will discuss forgiveness from many different angles. These ideas will extend past your marriage into many other relationships in your life. Realize your spouse also needs you to let go of your resentments toward them so the relationship can breathe.

Webster's defines forgiveness as, "To give up resentment of, or claim of requital, or to grant relief from payment of debt or personal injury."[1] Many things will happen over the course of your life that could cause resentment, bitterness, and a desire for revenge. But to live a full and successful life, you must develop the ability to let these go. I realize this is easier said than done sometimes. Scripture give us at least twenty-two different spiritual exercises to help us let go of toxic feelings. I think God gives us so many different instructions knowing we will experience all kinds of different hurts and difficulties during our life.

One of the most exciting bits of research I ran across in the last few years is from Dr. Don Partridge. He was researching the effect of divorce on children. He found that it was universally bad. Every study he did and every study he saw showed significant emotional damage on children because of their parent's divorce. In the midst of his research, however, he began running across a few individuals who were not affected by their parent's divorce; in fact, they were emotionally healthy. The first time he found one of these individuals, he was shocked and he interviewed this person. The young man had a unique philosophy about life and his parent's divorce. It consisted largely of five significant ideas. Dr. Partridge looked at this information as a complete random and outlier response.

A few years later, he ran across a woman who was also not affected negatively by her parent's divorce. When she was interviewed, she had the same five ideas that the first young man had. As Dr. Partridge continued doing his research, he found one of these healthy people every few years. They all had their own versions of the same five ideas. This was now becoming statistically significant. It has led to some ground-breaking therapies for children of divorce. Dr. Partridge put these ideas in his book, *Parent Wars: Dealing with an Ex to Raise Emotionally Healthy Kids*. Here are the five ideas that seemingly insulated the children from the damage of their parent's divorce.

1. I am on the same team as both of my parents—demonizing them is not productive.

2. I will deal with life as it is, not as I want it to be or what I think is fair.

3. I will forgive my parents for not being perfect parents and work with their strengths and weakness.

4. I will emphasize the positive about my parents and minimize the negative.

5. I will keep my family's secrets, sins, and confidences.[2]

These are some of the best expressions of how to live a life of forgiveness that I have ever seen. As I was listening to Dr. Partridge talk about these five key ideas, I personally realized that he was describing my own father's life philosophy. My father had been through his parents' bitter divorce back in the 1930s when no one got divorced. My father said all of these same ideas to me as I grew up. When I explained that this was a description of my father, Dr. Partridge told me that my father had given me a gift of immense value; he blessed me more than I can know.

My father had become an emotionally healthy adult because of these ideas and actions on forgiveness. My own life was spared by so many of the damages of bitterness. My father also modeled a life of forgiveness and love. Clearly these ideas apply to marriage as well as the rest of life. Take the time to apply these ideas to your parents and your spouse. Ask God to bring these truths into your life. Ask God to take away the bitterness.

I hope you caught the lesson here: all of us must develop tools to forgive—they have to be taught. The natural thing is to hold a grudge and allow resentments to build. I must say that forgiveness *does not* mean allowing a person who harms others to continue to do harm. But it *does* mean not allowing what someone else did to you to continue to haunt you for the rest of your life. *The ability to forgive is about building your future from where you are right now instead of allowing the other person to continue defining your future.* Yes, they may have done horrible things to you that are clearly wrong. And yes, they are a large part of the reason why you are where you are today. But it is essential to not let them control your future. You can choose to leave the past in the past and move forward with a new sense of purpose and zeal, as Paul talks about in Philippians 3:7–14.

There are three typical steps to take to get rid of resentments and get on with forgiveness. In one sense, it can be as easy as just "letting it go." Granted in reality, it is much harder than that. We often are so troubled, blocked, or redirected by what another person did to us that we have a hard time just letting it go. Maybe you were cheated in business; your husband or wife cheated on you; you were mentally, emotionally, or physically abused; you were injured in an accident; you were robbed of the promotion you should have gotten. If you are going to have a ridiculously great marriage, you will have to be able to forgive and let some things go. When you read this chapter, there may not be anything you need to forgive your spouse for and that is wonderful, but be prepared for when disappointments occur and resentments begin to enter into the joy of your marriage. Choose forgiveness instead of allowing your emotions to mix into a boiling cauldron of toxic waste.

I can remember a time early in my marriage when I was upset at my wife about some things she was not doing. I was driving toward town having this conversation with the Lord about the fact that I was very disappointed and wondered whether I would have to limp along with less than what I was hoping for in marriage. It was like God whispered that I needed to emphasize the positives, of which there were so many, and overlook the negatives, of which there were so few. I was making a mountain out of a few things, and it was growing bigger every day. "She is wonderful and you know it." Forgive her for not being perfect; you aren't either," is what He seemed to be saying. "Throw yourself into loving this wonderful woman and these small things will disappear."

I can honestly say that whatever those negative things were, they have completely disappeared. I don't have any idea what they are anymore. I find more joy, peace, and love in her presence than I ever thought was possible. Dana and I are a team, and good teammates make each other's weaknesses disappear. Now, let's look at these three steps toward forgiveness in detail.

THREE STEPS TO DEAL WITH TOXIC EMOTIONS

Every ridiculously great marriage has some system of forgiving the other person. Here are my simple steps: 1) Process your toxic emotions; 2) Neutralize your toxic emotions; 3) Release your toxic emotions. Sometimes you can work through these steps quickly, and sometimes they take quite a while. There are a number of great books and deeper dives into forgiveness and/or dealing with toxic emotions. I would highly recommend them: *Total Forgiveness* by R.T. Kendall, *Celebrate Recovery*, any of Dr. Don Partridge's books, and Dr. Daniel *Amen's* books on dealing with toxic emotions.

It is clear from Jesus's comments about forgiveness in the Lord's Prayer and in Matthew 18 that we are not designed to hold on to bitterness, anger, or hatred. We need to release them to God and others. I am going to give you a brief description of each step and then a few practical exercises to work through that step.

1. **Process the toxic emotions.**

   Many of us are so disconnected from our own feelings, we don't really know what we feel; or we can be so accustomed to suppressing our emotions, we don't feel anything at all—we're numb. This is extremely unhealthy mentally, emotionally, spiritually, and relationally. Our emotions can be powerful indicators of things gone wrong. When we suppress them or don't deal with them at all, we won't live our best lives. We can process our emotions by learning to understand, make sense of, and deal with them in healthy, productive ways. It takes time to identify and process what we feel, but when we do, then we can deal with them. Here are two spiritual exercises to help you do this.

Spiritual Exercise: Bring the negative emotions into the light.

We have to get the toxic emotions out of our heads—they just get more toxic if we leave negative thoughts or feelings swirling around inside. This means talking about our emotions and what happened with a safe person, writing about it in a journal, or praying to God about it. In a sense, we are taking these negative emotions from deep within our subconsciousness and bringing them out through our soul (mind, will, and emotions), then out through our body (through talking, writing, singing, praying, creating, and so forth). Bitterness, depression, anger, and hatred can build up for many reasons, so if we are going to keep these negative emotions from overwhelming us, we need to work through why they happened, how they happened, what happened, and what is happening to us because of them. We need to bring these emotions from deep within us to outside of us in some way.

There is something important about not letting our negative emotions remain unexamined inside of us. Jesus tells us, "Blessed are those who mourn, for they shall be comforted" (Matt. 5:4). Start figuring out what mourning looks like for you. How do you get your negative emotions outside of your body, outside of your own head? Who can you talk with? Who is a safe person who will talk about what you are going through and feeling? What creative outlets can help you with this process? Can you write down what you are feeling? Can you paint it or sing about it?

I can remember so many times talking with my youth pastor or a trusted mentor about situations and feelings and them giving me a completely different perspective about the situation. Their new perspectives gave me a whole new set of emotions and new ways of coping with the situations in my life.

Take some time to walk in a nearby park and pray to God about what you are feeling and thinking. I have worn off the bark on some of the trees in the park near my house through my loud and strong prayers dealing with the various situations in my life. Remember we have to get our feelings outside of our own head. We have to be open to new perspectives and new ideas, which will not happen if we are not authentic and real about life.

Buy a little notebook and write down what you are thinking and feeling to get the thoughts and emotions outside of your body. Many times, it is the movement of pen to paper that makes a huge difference in our overall mental health. It seems like a small thing, but it really does help. The scientists tell us that writing down our emotions makes us access a different part of our brain, and this helps us process emotions and ideas. We don't need another TV show or movie or distraction putting thoughts into our mind; we need to get some of the thoughts in our mind out via paper, people, and prayer.

Spiritual Exercise: Ask questions about your negative emotions.

One of the best ways to process your emotions is to ask and answer questions about what you are feeling and wanting to do. If you have a friend who can ask you questions and probe your thoughts and feelings, great! But you can probe on your own, too, using the questions below. Write your answers down in a journal (keep it hidden), and ask and answer these questions with God through prayer. Don't just keep thinking the same thoughts and feeling the same outrage...process what is going on within you. Fully digest what happened so you can move past this incident. Don't let an injustice define you. Overcome it by processing it.

What happened from my perspective?

What happened from the other person's perspective?

Why did it happen, both from my perspective and from their perspective?

How did it happen? What led up to this incident, interaction, or indignation?

When I think about this incident or issue, what comes to mind?

How does my perspective make me feel?

How does the other person's perspective make them feel?

What have I chosen to do about this issue?

What have I chosen to do with my negative emotions?

Does my anger, depression, bitterness, hatred, and other negative emotions stem from an expectation I have or had for the other person?

Is that expectation realistic?

Was the expectation clearly communicated?

Is the expectation fair to the other person?

Are they really capable of meeting my expectations given who they are, how they were raised, or where they currently are in their life?

Is there another way of looking at this situation?

How can I think about this issue and see it as a small thing?

Who do I need to share my thoughts, choices, and feelings with?

2. **Neutralize the toxic emotions.**

Just like scientists neutralize poisons by mixing in new chemicals, we need to add in new things to the negative emotions that naturally erupt in our minds. After we have a clear picture of what the toxicity is really all about, then we can add new elements to these ideas. How can God use this to start something new? What can be done to get past this issue? How can we make sure this never happens again?

Spiritual Exercise: Mix in new thoughts and perspectives.

In this exercise, we neutralize the emotion by combining it with other ideas and thoughts, so we can see it from a new perspective. Prayerfully ask,

Are there any ways this incident can be seen as a good thing?

Are there any ways that good can come out of this issue, incident, or injustice?

Who can I talk to for a new or different perspective, not to take my side, but to help me see things in a new or different way or reframe the incident or situation?

What materials can I read that might give me new insights?

What does Scripture say about my emotions or situation?

Spiritual Exercise: Add goodness to their lives.

Jesus says to love your enemies, do good to those who use you, and bless those who curse you (Matt. 5:43–48). These are instructions for how to neutralize your negative emotions by adding something really good and righteous to the mix. It is amazing how this works. Let me give you a few examples.

I can remember a time when I was so upset at my wife over something. She was attending a class, and I was home with the kids. I was growing impatient and was just waiting for when she would come home so I could unload on her about how she was wrong. In the midst of this stewing and toxicity, the Holy Spirit brought this strange idea to my mind. *Buy her a gift.* I argued back, insisting that I didn't want to reward the behavior I was so mad about. But the promptings of the Holy Spirit would not stop. So I packed up the girls and we drove into town to buy their mom some new slippers and a robe. All the way into town I was thinking about how this was a really stupid idea. But all the way back from town I was excited about presenting her a gift and talking with the girls about how wonderful their mom was. The negative emotion had been neutralized by combining it with doing a good thing for my wife. Romans 12:21 says, "Do not be overcome by evil, but overcome evil with good." The wisdom in this passage is profound.

> *What goodness can I add to my spouse's life to neutralize my negative emotions and bring peace and joy to our relationship?*

> *What is the Holy Spirit prompting me to do, even now?*

This idea extends far beyond just the relationship you have with your spouse. It works with your kids, work colleagues, and neighbors. I remember a father who came to see me about the issues his young teenage son was facing and embracing. The father was appalled that his son was considering a completely different lifestyle than their Christian family. The father had been a strict, loving, and busy father, who wanted the best for his family. He was getting upset and filled with emotion as he told me about what his son was contemplating.

I suggested that much of a young person's anger and issues come from distance between them and their father, and I recommended that he add lots more time with his son doing all kinds of fun things, having great discussions, and so forth. This was a way to neutralize what he was feeling and potentially neutralize a lot of what that young man was feeling.

Three months later, I ran into the father and he was beaming. The man and his son were spending a lot of time together and the troubling feelings that the father and the boy were experiencing were completely gone. It was a delightful, growing relationship.

So many marriages fall apart because everything else in life is allowed to take time away from the marriage. I remember saying to one man, "I can't fix your marriage unless you change jobs or move closer to your current job. Both of you have so many emotional issues with each other, and what you really need is about one to two hours a day spent talking, hanging out, having fun, and relaxing, which right now goes into your commute." The couple acted on my advice and they moved into an apartment five minutes from his work. This was like a magic elixir on their marriage. They had neutralized the bitterness in order to spend more time together.

3. **Release the toxic emotions.**

In the verses that make up the Lord's Prayer, Jesus asks us to talk with God on a daily basis about who we should forgive, "And forgive us our debts as we have also forgiven our debtors" (Matt. 6:12). We need to release them and ourselves from the toxic emotions. We can choose to let go of the toxic emotions by letting go of the offense and releasing them to God and their own life.

Spiritual Exercise—Drop your keys.

Whenever I speak on this topic, I explain that our resentments are like our keys we hold in our hands. Keys dig into our palms and are not comfortable to just hold on to. So bitterness constantly pokes at us, hurts us, and draws attention to itself. Just drop the injustice, let it go, and stop trying to get fairness. Forgiveness is like the act of dropping your keys and walking away. (I will usually drop my keys on stage in a dramatic fashion and walk away from them.)

If I continue to hang on to those resentments, I cannot move into the future. I must *choose* to no longer hold the person liable for the things they did. They may be liable to the state, to the Lord, to the company, or whatever, but I will no longer be looking for or taking advantage of opportunities to pay them back. I'm letting them go.

I talk to the Lord everyday about people I need to forgive. I allow Him to speak to me about whether I have dropped my resentments toward my spouse, neighbor, boss, parents, and so forth. He'll usually tell me a name of someone if I have picked up my keys again. I tell God I want to move into the future from where I am. I may not be able to go back to where I was before they did what they did, but I want to move into the future. I want to separate myself from them by forgiving them.

Begin by saying to God and to yourself, "I forgive _____ for what they did to me, and I will no longer look for opportunities to pay them back.

I want to forge into the future and embrace all you have for me." It may take a number of days and a few spiritual exercises until God no longer brings up their name, but don't give up. Ask, "Lord, is there anyone who I have not forgiven, since you have forgiven me so much?" This is God's will for you, so He will see it through.

Inevitably, we tend to pick up our resentments again—our keys. There are times when I have to repeat my declarations of forgiveness because the keys end up back in my hand without me even realizing I picked them up again. Believe it or not, this is a test to see if I am really willing to forgive them. Will I focus on the future and not the past? Will I drop those keys again?

Spiritual Exercise—Hire God as your hit man.

One of the best ways to release our negative emotions is to give them over to God to take care of the issues of vengeance and punishment. Our ideas and perspectives of what is the right amount of vengeance and punishment are always colored by our passions and limits. God says we are not equipped to handle vengeance, but He is. He knows what a person really deserves and needs, and He know their heart. He can be trusted with doing what is needed. I call this "hiring God as your hitman." Look at the verses in Romans 12:19–20,

> *Never take your own revenge, beloved, but leave room*
> *for the wrath of God, for it is written, "Vengeance is mine,*
> *I will repay," says the Lord. "But if your enemy is hungry,*
> *feed him, and if he is thirsty, give him a drink; for in*
> *doing so you will heap burning coals on his head."*

Spiritual Exercise—Leave the past behind and focus on the future.

This spiritual exercise is really useful to drop our resentments once and for all. God tells us about this exercise through the inspired statements of the apostle Paul in the book of Philippians, "But one thing I do: forgetting what lies behind and reaching forward to what lies ahead, I press on toward the goal for the prize of the upward call of God in Christ Jesus" (Phil. 3:13–14).

Focusing on the future involves goals, plans, and action. One of the only ways to conquer our resentments, bitterness, and desire for revenge is to go after our goals. If your anger at what someone did to you is so strong that you have no goals except to see them paid back, then this is a signal to you that your resentments have created a prison in which you now live in. Break out of this prison by forgiving the person and stretching toward the life God has for you. There are lots of positive things you can do, and it will require all that you are and much of God's grace to accomplish them.

One way I focus on the future is by asking God the question, "What could I be doing three to five years from now that I am not doing now?" I use the basic relational list to help me focus on my future. I ask God to give me insights, ideas, and goals for how to make each area of my life better. "God, what can my ideal marriage (family, work, finances, and so forth) look like in three to five years? What can I do now to begin moving toward those goals?"

Listen for and trust God's answer as Proverbs 3:5–6 says to "Trust in the Lord with all your heart, and do not lean on your own understanding. In all your ways acknowledge him, and he will make your paths straight." And Proverbs 20:24 NIV, "A person's steps are directed by the Lord. How then can anyone understand their own way?"

We all know what it feels like when someone holds something we've done or said against us. I don't try to hurt my wife, but sometimes I do. If she was not the type of person who was quick to forgive, I don't know what I'd do. I do know there would be a lot of added pain and tension in the relationship, and I am thankful for the way we both forgive one another more freely now. Letting go of resentments allows the grace of God to do its work. Whenever someone does something against me, I can't help but think, "There but for the grace of God go I."[3] It could have just as easily been me doing the offending. We all have faults and make mistakes, so it is best to quickly forgive, especially your spouse. That's what makes a marriage ridiculously great. I hope these exercises and ideas will help you move away from a marriage of toxicity and into a marriage of forgiveness.

Habit #12

Align Your Expectations

"Can two people walk together without agreeing on the direction?"

(Amos 3:3 NLT)

I recently had a conversation with a couple about their vacation, which was clearly headed towards disaster. Both the husband and the wife were thinking, expecting, and excited about completely different things. They had not discussed their different perspectives or goals, what they wanted to do, how much they wanted to spend…they were both just planning to force what they wanted to happen onto the other one.

I knew it was going to be a train wreck, because this couple did not know how to align their expectations. Inevitably, they would spring their desires on their spouse at a time when it seemed like the other person couldn't say no. They would both get sad, angry, sexy, or whatever their success strategy had been in the past when they might not get their way. The vacation would have a huge fight or internal aggravation in the midst of it. But it didn't have to be this way.

Do you find yourself wondering why nothing really works out the way you want it to? This habit teaches how to align your expectations before events, plans, and activities, so your marriage doesn't descend into unnecessary fights. The alignment exercise in this chapter can save much heartache and pain.

Everyone has wishes, expectations, and desires. That's a given in life. Most people can let go of wishes and desires if they are not met, but once something has hardened into an expectation, that's when everything changes. Most apologies could begin with the phrase, "I'm sorry but I expected _____ to happen, and when it didn't, I got upset."

Expectations are the key to a great time or a lousy time. This is why it is important to find a way to talk about expectations before things happen. Let me relate this idea to the business world. A friend of mine explained to me that one of the ways he increased productivity and staff morale at a company he consulted was to have employees write down what they thought they were supposed to do in the next week, from most important to least important. This was to be a detailed list of what they were going to do in the next five days.

He also had the supervisors write down what they wanted the employees to do from most important to least important. It was amazing to compare the lists. They were never the same. The expectations between employees and supervisors at underperforming companies were always different and there was no time set aside to get on the same page. My friend scheduled thirty minutes at the beginning of every day so that employees and supervisors could compare expectations. Productivity, praise, and staff morale shot up every time. If it is this way in a company, it is even truer in a marriage.

Learn the lesson of this business consultant. Before you and your spouse blindly head into the weekend, evening, vacation, work week, or spending the bonus money, align your expectations to uncover what you both hope and expect to happen. Ask your spouse what they are hoping, expecting, and bracing for in these coming events. If you are willing to listen and share, your marriage will change significantly for the better.

With hidden expectations and wishes out in the open, change can happen because there is enough time and information to make the changes. The two of you will not always be able to accommodate everything each other is saying, but you can discuss how you will adjust the event or activity to meet as much of the expectations as possible. This means being willing to declare what you hope will happen and listen to what the other person hopes will happen. Then a willingness to think through ways to include each other's ideas, adjust schedules and activities as appropriate, and/or find a third alternative the two of you had not considered before. This is what a couple with a ridiculously great marriage does. They make a concerted effort to align their expectations for all sorts of things.

REMEMBER THE WIN-WIN

Too many couples approach these crucial times or life events with a view of getting what they want individually. But that creates a situation where it will be a win for one person and a loss for the other person, which is not a trait of a ridiculously great marriage. There is always a way to create a win-win opportunity out of something that was going to be a win-lose situation. If both of you are committed to looking for the wise use of the time, money, and energy, there is some option that is really good for everyone. This is along the same vein as habit #10—*Making Decisions Together.*

Going back to habit #6—*Seek Wisdom, Not Your Own Way,* this kind of thinking is "wisdom." Wisdom is becoming more and more rare in a world of five hundred channels of television, unlimited YouTube videos, Ted Talks, and social media. Our world has become so segmented that each person is able to find something specifically delightful to them with little thought of whether it is interesting, helpful, or enjoyable to anyone else. We often don't need to compromise anymore to enjoy a broader fun that includes more people. We tend to know exactly what we want to do and refuse to settle for something less than what we want. But in marriage, this doesn't work.

One couple I know of made the mistake of settling into time-consuming hobbies—separately. He got into motorcycles and spent much of his weekends taking long rides or working on his bikes, and she got into training for and competing in triathlons. There was no discussion about what the expectations were for each of them as it related to the marriage and spending time together—it was all so separate, they ended up divorcing. Perhaps if they had spent some time aligning their expectations, asking questions, and listening to each other, they could have come to a place of support rather than having competing interests. Or maybe they would have found some things to do together. Sadly, this happens more often than not. There is a way to build a ridiculously great marriage together, but you must work at it. Aligning expectations is some of that work.

The process is fairly simple—listening to the other person's ideas, expectations, and dreams about how to spend a period of time or how to spend some money or expend some energy. If they are not sharing, then ask questions to draw out what they are thinking. When it's their turn to listen to you, state your expectations about the same period of time, spending the same money, and expending the same energy. I say to my wife all the time, "There are always options. I just need to know what you are thinking and expecting, and we can find something that will work for both of us."

Sometimes, when you or your partner first state what you are expecting to do with the weekend or a vacation, for example, there will often be a sense of doom when it is first communicated. This is because it might be so different from what you were expecting to do with the same money, time, or energy. This is normal. Just don't let it stay within that doomsday mentality. Keep listening and be willing to say what you were expecting and why. There is a way toward the wise choice.

I had to laugh the other day as my wife and I were discussing a day off we were planning. I got really quiet and she asked me why I was so quiet. I told her I was dreading one of the things that we had agreed to do the next day, and I was looking for a way out of doing it. She was shocked because she was looking forward to it. But we both talked about ways to keep it from being as bad as I was expecting. I had to go, but having her understand my feelings and expectations allowed me to get through the hated event relatively unscathed.

This process of aligning expectations is one of the greatest tools for marriage harmony. It is so much better than waiting until you are in the middle of the weekend only to discover you have differing expectations, not to mention the fights, anger, or significant moodiness that go along with it.

Anger and Unmet Expectations

One of the issues with anger is that it is largely tied to unrealistic or unmet expectations. The expectation may be "right" or "moral" or "normal," but it is unrealistic given the finances, the state of the relationship, the other person, the circumstances, the kids, or a hundred other things. Sometimes an expectation is unrealistic because it was not properly communicated. It is as if your spouse was just supposed to read your mind and know to do something or not do something.

One of the things about aligning expectations is it gets what's expected out in the open before the event happens. Many expectations could be seen as unrealistic once they are out in the open—that's the beauty of it. It just sounds off. Just saying it out loud causes the person to back off on the expectation.

Ever since my wife and I learned this simple exercise, it has been so helpful to us. Dana will say, "What are your expectations about this weekend?" Or, "What do you think we should do with this money?" Or, "How do you think we should deal with this situation with one of the girls?" Or, "You are so wise when it comes to these situations, what do you think we should do?" These and many others are her way of hearing what my expectations are for that situation.

I will sometimes want to hear her point of view before I share mine. Sometimes she really wants to hear mine before she shares hers. We have avoided hundreds of disagreements and hurt feelings by aligning our expectations way before we are in the situation that would naturally trigger a blow-up.

Getting Practical

Think of an issue or situation or event that is coming where you can discuss what the other person is expecting to happen. It can be helpful to start with non-emotional issues so it won't lead a fight. You can begin the conversation by saying something like,

> *Can we align our expectations about this weekend/paycheck/vacation?*
>
> *Let's both discuss what we see us doing.*
>
> *What do you want to accomplish?*
>
> *What are the options to get the most done and have it become the wisest use of our time/money/resources?*
>
> *What would you like to see come out of this time/energy/money?*

Be willing to hear the other person out. Don't interrupt with your changes until they are finished. You might bring up an objection to their expectation with a question like, "What are we going to do about …?" Or maybe a positive statement like, "I would love to do that but I am not sure it will work with the need to pick up the kids back at the school," or whatever.

Just be careful not to shut down the other person's expectations—allow them to get it all out there, then try and find a way they fit together. At times, it may be obvious that everybody's expectations can't be met. Have a discussion before the event; it can be resolved much easier than if you wait until the event or circumstance is happening.

It is the hidden expectations that often sink a relationship—one's that aren't vocalized and assumed. Yes, sometimes a person doesn't get their expectations met, but it should not always be the same person who sacrifices their plan. There has to be a give and take. Possible options are always out there, and usually, there is a way to meet many expectations if you are creative.

Aligning expectations can become a part of the regular staff meeting, or in some cases, it might need to be a daily thing or case-by-case. If you do choose to address these at the staff meeting, then both spouses can add to the list of things to be aligned. Here's what an agenda item might look like for you:

Aligning expectations:

> *Husband and/or wife's paycheck*
>
> *This weekend*
>
> *Daughter's weekend*
>
> *Saturday morning*

Church this week

Fishing trip with the guys

Date night on Sunday

Dinner on Friday because of football game

It would do each spouse some good to think about what their expectations are—write them down or voice them aloud. Give some thought about how you want your home life to be like. How do you expect the children to act? What should mealtimes be like? How should this Saturday go? What should I be doing and everyone else be doing when family comes to visit?

For me, it's pretty basic. I like peace in my home. I like when my wife is excited to see me. I like when me, my wife, and children have a pretty good idea of what is coming next in life. I like it when everybody is happy. The way I keep things going well is by aligning expectations. This habit will help you avoid problems and create a ridiculously happy marriage.

Set Regular Budget Meetings

Among the top reasons why couples divorce, money issues rank consistently within the top five. Divorce proceedings often cite incompatibility, finances, lack of love, communication, and distrust. You don't win against this negative list by attacking them directly; you win by practicing the habits in this book.

Money may be a huge problem area in marriage, but it's not usually the lack of money that causes the divorce. Rather, it is the lack of *compatibility* about how to handle money that causes the problems. Opposites may attract, but when two people are opposites in the financial department, wounds, wars, and divorce can follow. Imagine the conflict if one is a saver and one is a spender. One is focused on the future, while the other believes in living for today. One has no problem buying on credit, while the other believes in saving up. Over time, this conflict can reach such heights that divorce seems to be the only logical conclusion.

Why do couples struggle so much in the financial arena? It is because they do not have a simple way of discussing and deciding how to handle their money.

In this book, I am making the case that by adopting a few simple habits, you can build a ridiculously great marriage. And since so many couples struggle in this area, I wanted to make sure to introduce a habit that will help make money issues less stressful and more manageable. Let me introduce you to habit #13—*Set Regular Budget Meetings*.

MAKE BUDGETING A TEAM APPROACH

I am amazed at the number of couples who don't approach finances as a team. One person or the other makes all the decisions. This may help you budget, but it doesn't necessarily help the marriage. As you work together and build a financial life both of you can live with, your marriage will be on the right track. At one time, my wife and I were no different. When we first got married, I was an extremely cautious spender and strong saver, and my wife was more of a spender. I could make a dollar really sweat by budgeting it to the nth degree. I came to realize that forcing my wife to adopt my budgeting ways was not the best way to make our marriage or finances work.

At one point, I remember praying, "God, I know she deserves more than what I can provide right now. If you want to provide more, I will use it to bless her and still be financially sound." Almost immediately, God began increasing my salary and outside speaking opportunities. I changed the budget to bless her and was able to fill out the categories throughout the whole budget. God has regularly blessed us as a family out of the blue with unexpected bonuses, checks, and extra work opportunities to make everybody in the house breathe easier. I am grateful for His faithfulness and goodness to us, but we work together by holding regular budget meetings. It's a team effort, one we are faithful to keep.

When my wife and I first started holding our budget meetings, we initially met every week. Then once we got the system down, we began to meet monthly. We needed extra time to discuss finances, so we started having a meeting every time we got a check of any kind. Now we're back to weekly meetings. We have found that aligning our expectations on a weekly basis to discuss purchases for that week has created discussions rather than reasons for apologizing.

Each of us has our weekly duties in regards to the finances, and we have a review meeting right before the end of the month or at the beginning of the next month. We ask questions such as, how do we want the next month to unfold financially? How much do we want to save? How much spending will we allow in a particular category? What are the unexpected expenses that typically come up this time of year? Your schedule will be different than ours, but you need to have one, so that the spending plan is above board for each week or each month.

BUDGET WITH UNITY IN MIND

If you are just getting started, I would suggest you make budget issues a part of every staff meeting to promote unity, which we talked about in habit #2— *Hold a Weekly Staff Meeting.* You can discuss what is probably going to be spent, the spending limits, what needs to be postponed because of the budget, what you are saving towards, what any new income will go towards, and so on. This consolidates time and focus.

It is very common, these days, for couples to have too many bills, too many wants, and too many dreams for the money they make. The advertising companies make sure that we always want more than we can afford. Many couples have the idea their marriage should have enough money for many, if not all, of their desires, as well as their spouse's. This is fantasyland. I know couples who make over $300,000 a year but are barely making it (and I have heard of couples making over $800,000 per year arguing and fighting over money). Sounds insane, I know! Why are they struggling so much? Simple. They have given into all of their wants and desires. They need a budget, and they need to stick to it.

When they begin to budget with a design for *harmony and peace,* their marriage will settle down. A simple budget allows a couple to start working together instead of against one another. Unless you inculcate sound biblical principles into your money management systems, your marriage could be destroyed over money matters.

DEVELOP A BIBLICAL MONEY SYSTEM

Our current American culture does not teach helpful principles about the financial arena. In many cases, we are taught destructive ideas that will eventually lead to financial ruin and relational devastation. The Bible is a great guide with ancient principles for handling money wisely. For the scope of this project, I won't be able to get into great depth, but I will lay out some key principles to guide your thinking on biblical money management. Money doesn't have to become an explosive issue for your marriage.

Great marriages have some sort of biblical system for money allocation that allows couples to make money in righteous ways, spend in predictable ways, save for the future, and have enough money to last all month with some left to give. We can break this down into four basic categories to guide your financial life: *income, money management, savings, and generosity.*

Even if finances are not an area of strength for you, it is important to have at least a basic knowledge of biblical principles in these four areas. Let's take a look at each of these.

Income

Say you are a couple who struggles with the income side of finances. It feels like you are working as hard as you can, but you don't make enough to pay the bills (or maybe you do but your expenses are out of whack). By learning God's income principles, you can determine if you need more streams of income, if there is a productivity issue with how you make your money, or if there is a more God-honoring way to make money. Sometimes both spouses need to work to bring in enough income to make ends meet or accomplish certain goals. Sometimes it actually saves money for one spouse to not work outside the home to focus on keeping expenses under control, as in the case of childrearing, at least for a time. Decide what income solutions work best for your situation and commit to them.

Money Management

Most couples need to learn God's principles for managing money because they have enough money (even though it doesn't seem like it), but they are not allocating it well (Prov. 27:23–27). But do you realize you have the power and ability to *tell your money what you want it to do?* One of the biggest money management principles is to not spend more than you make. This would seem obvious, but it isn't in our day and age of instant gratification and 24/7 advertising. Plan on spending less than you bring in every month, and in a little while, you will have reserves and margins to work with.

It begins with a basic budget. Start with your gross income, which has taxes, benefits, and retirement taken out before you see any of the money. The amount left is what you have to deal with—your net spendable income. Here are some sample percentages per category that can be a starting point for figuring out where your money should go:

RECOMMENDED SPENDING CATEGORIES

Tithe	10%	Recreation	7%
Housing	32%	Clothing	5%
Food	10%	Medical	5%
Automobiles	10%	Savings	5%
Debts	5%	Miscellaneous	5%
Insurance	5%		

Totals 100% of your net, spendable income

Starting with percentages of your net income is so much better than starting with what you want. What you want has to fit into what you have, or you will become deeply in debt, or worse—broke. Yes, you will have to limit yourself in some categories to make any budget work. For my wife and me, one of the rules for money we established early was that we would prepare a budget and then let the budget decide if we could spend money on something. If there was money in the budget, then we would do it; but if it wasn't there, then we couldn't no matter who wanted it or how badly they desired it. Keeping to the budget definitely requires self-control and teamwork, but God gives us His Spirit of self-control in all areas, including finances (Gal. 5:23).

These areas where you need to limit yourself and find creative options are opportunities for creative conversations in the marriage. If you do not have these discussions together, then you will most likely blame the other person for why you don't get what you want. Let me say there is almost never enough money to go around, no matter how much you make. Yes, you may have unique circumstances and your budget will look completely different, but you need to have budget discussions. The most important question to begin with is, "What do we want this money to do before we get our next check?" This will go a long way to help you and your spouse get on the same page financially. If you talk regularly and have a reasonable financial understanding, your budget will be a road map to financial peace.

Many times, these overall discussions happen best right before a raise, bonus, or change in employment. If you make a change with new money, then you don't miss it when it goes for savings, retirement, and emergency funds. I can remember having discussions with Dana before a particular job was going to pay us significantly less than we had been making. We had lots of conversations about what would have to be sacrificed and what was crucial. We have also had a number of discussions right before raises kicked in to plan how we would make the new money work for us instead of just disappear into a larger lifestyle. The key is communication.

If you want to go a little deeper into the budgeting process, I have provided three plans to help you think about the overall budget. Take a look at each of them and decide which system could work best for you given your goals, needs, and income.

80–10–10 Plan

This is where you plan on spending only 80 percent of what lands in your hands, you save 10 percent of what lands in your hands, and you give 10 percent of what lands in your hands away. This is the spending and budgeting plan most people start with. This means you add up everything that comes into your marriage as income, and you take 80 percent of it to spend on bills, fun, miscellaneous, and no more. Ten percent of what comes in will be sent into a retirement program or savings at the bank or some kind of savings account, then the remaining 10 percent will be given away to charity—the church, non-profit organizations, and so forth. It is assumed that your taxes are taken out before you see the money. If you are self-employed, you must take out 25–35 percent for taxes before you start the 80–10–10 plan.

70–20–10 Plan

This is where you spend only 70 percent of what lands in your hands after taxes have been taken out. You arrange your budget to only spend that much. The total of the categories must be 70 percent or less. There are software apps (YNAB, Mint, and others) that are so helpful, because they will really help you stay on track with each category and the total amount you have to spend. You will send 20 percent of what lands in your hands to a retirement account or savings plan. Remember, you only really have what you pay yourself. In this plan, it is 20 percent of what comes in as net income. Ten percent is still reserved for church, charity, and good works in your world. There is something powerful that happens when people honor God and care for the poor as they are prospering.

50–20–10–10–10 Plan

This is the plan that causes many people to move ahead very quickly to reach their financial goals, get out of the rat race, and into financial freedom and high impact. This is where you and your spouse agree to spend only 50 percent of what lands in your hands (net income). Twenty percent of your net income is invested in retirement, savings, and investments. Ten percent is given to your church as a tithe to make the ministry move forward and honor God. Ten percent is given to the poor through various organizations or directly to them. In the Old Testament, this was called a poor tax. It is not mandatory on New Testament Christians, but it is a hedge against an over focus on money, materialism, and a wealthy lifestyle. It allows significant resources to be directed to particular worthy causes outside of the church. The final 10 percent is set aside for an emergency fund so that three months to one year's worth of funds can be built up to handle emergencies and any period of job change or unemployment.

Savings/Investments

It is prudent to save between 10 to 20 percent of your net income for retirement, investments, and savings for when you can't work. At some time in the future, you may not be able to work, so you will need to have a nest egg that will allow you to live and not be a burden on your parents, children, or the community. Too many people are dependent on the country or their company, and they are being disappointed. Set aside 10+ percent of your income for your future. Yes, I know that it means you will have to cut back on some of the things you want right now, but you will really thank me when you have a growing nest egg. Then, you don't have to stay in a dead-end job forever, or you can look for a better job because you know you are not stuck.

Generosity

Many couples do not understand the absolute need for generosity if our society, marriages, and children are to be healthy. Notice I have a generosity piece in every financial plan above, because one does not get ahead with a stingy attitude. There must be a generosity plan of some kind for your finances to work. We must be people who are generous—with each other, with those who are less fortunate, with our community of faith, and so on. Yes, you will have to sacrifice in some ways to be generous, but it will be worth it. The generous people are the people whose marriages work really well. God can bless us more when we are generous with what He gives us.

THE BUDGET MEETING

As a couple, you can really begin to inoculate yourself against divorce due to money issues by having a budget meeting to align expectations and get on the same page. A budget meeting should occur weekly or at least every time you get a paycheck, which for most couples would be at the beginning and middle of the month.

One of the most helpful disciplines my wife and I got into was to ask each other what we wanted this money to do until the next time we got a check. At first, we had completely different ideas, and the discussions were fascinating. There were times when we had to put off what one person wanted to do until the next pay period in order to meet an immediate, higher-priority need in the present paycheck window. We heard each other out and worked towards the priorities, wisdom, and delights of both people. Agreement came easier and easier over time.

Talk as a couple and come to an agreement about what you want that money to do. Regular income usually gets designated for regular expenses, such as rent/mortgage, utilities, and so forth, but it is always good to acknowledge you have the right to say what you want the money to do. If you don't do this, then your money will usually be spent in ways that are wasteful or random. If you can't agree about how to spend the money, put it straight into savings until you can agree. You may need to make a list of things the money can do, such as pay off a specific bill, buy something for the home, build an emergency fund to act as a buffer, put some aside for an upcoming expense, and so forth. Between the two of you, all of the things the money can be used for will become apparent. Then you just have to figure out which one is the best use of that money.

When you first begin meeting like this about money, it could take an hour or longer. After a while, you and your spouse will be able to come to agreement in less than five to ten minutes, in most cases. Budget meetings should be positive and future focused, not punitive and backward looking. Ask, "Where are we going to aim the funds we have just received for maximum, positive impact for the whole family?" Realize both spouses may have very different ideas on how to spend the money that comes into the family. This is great. Just have a discussion and find wisdom where everybody wins in some way.

Simply ask, "We just got our normal paycheck. What do we want this money to do until the next one comes in?" If you aren't deliberate about this, there will always be more things to spend money on than money to spend. More money is not always the answer. I have seen people earning almost a million dollars a year, who struggle with how they are going to get all they want with that much money. Conversely, I have seen couples who make $24,000 a year combined doing extremely well, because they have agreed where every dollar goes. It all comes down to three things:

how well you can work together;

agreeing on where it should be spent;

following through to make sure it is spent in the agreed-upon way.

EMPLOY GOOD BUDGETING TOOLS AND RESOURCES

There are some great tools and educational materials that can really educate people on how to make a budget work. These tools make a huge difference in getting on the same page financially. A number of years ago, I was teaching a group of about 150 men on the power of budgeting. I mentioned a number of mobile apps that can help a person budget. A few months later, a man came and thanked me for recommending the use of one of the mobile apps. Since he had started using it to help manage his money, he and his wife were no longer living paycheck to paycheck. In fact, he had saved a whole month's worth of money as a buffer.

I was not using the one he had mentioned, and I was intrigued by how quickly this mobile app had changed his family's finances. I soon switched to the one he was using because of its ability to help both my wife and myself comprehend budgeting in a way that made sense to both of us. In fact, one of the first principles this mobile app teaches is, "When you get a check, have a meeting."

You Need a Budget, or Y.N.A.B. (www.ynab.com), is the mobile app I recommend using, because it walks you through the various categories of a typical budget, subtracting the amount you commit to a category from the total left to budget. It forces you to commit together where every dollar is going to go until the next paycheck comes in. Those arranged amounts show up on your phone app and keep track in real time what you have left in a category. I have consistently seen couples who started using Y.N.A.B. stop living paycheck to paycheck within a few weeks or a few months. It really is amazing. There are hundreds of podcast tutorials for learning the software, and the budgeting ideas at their website are free. I can't recommend it enough.

Another financial tool I highly recommend is the *Financial Peace University* educational programs by Dave Ramsey, which can be found at many churches and online. This program is especially helpful at getting couples out of debt and into stable thinking about money and financial expectations. There is a tremendous amount of financial illiteracy in our country, so these classes are very helpful. Many couples take the course multiple times to deeply embrace and incorporate the principles into their lives, and they should. I always recommend that young married couples or engaged couples should start their marriage off right by taking these courses. It really can help avoid a lot of conflict later down the road.

Keep Talking, Keep Communicating, Keep Meeting

Some couples or individuals are highly complacent about money. They want the money side of a marriage to magically take care of itself. It won't. You have to work together with agreed upon goals to accomplish what you want your finances to do. Even if you hate talking about money, you need to talk with your spouse about what you want your dollars to do every time a check comes in. Even if your spouse handles the money, both of you need to interact about what you want this new money that just came in to do. This is the bare minimum.

Remember these guidelines for budgeting:

1. Once a week or when you get a check, hold a meeting.

2. Examine expenditures. Figure out where every dollar goes to determine where your spending percentages are currently. Then using the "Recommended Spending Categories" table, decide what areas are out of balance and which ones are in the normal range. Now you can see what expenses to adjust in your spending plan.

3. Decide on what kind of spending plan you want to adhere to and go from there. Will the 80–10–10 work better for you, the 70–20–10, or the 50–20–10–10–10?

4. Integrate budgeting decisions and track spending by engaging in budgeting software, such as YNAB or another one you like, so you can keep much better track of where you are financially in real time.

5. Stay committed to your budget meetings and the process—you'll be amazed at how much progress you will make in your finances if you do.

Stop Fighting, Start Learning and Discussing

In marriage, there are bound to be concerns, complaints, or issues that come up where you and your spouse disagree. One spouse gets annoyed, the other may be oblivious, but something needs to change. Fights mainly happen because too much emotion is involved; too much "this is what I want" or "this is how you hurt me" factor in. How can you share these offending matters with each other without it escalating into a blame game or shutting down altogether? How can you promote change with someone you love in an effective, God-honoring way?

This is what habit #14 is all about—*Stop Fighting, Start Learning and Discussing*. If your spouse has something to say, let them say it. Try to understand what they are saying rather than reacting to the emotion they are saying it with.

I have recently dealt with a number of couples who fight so much it seems the marriage is headed towards separation or divorce. In almost every case, the couples seem to have no "ground rules" or "rules of engagement" when one spouse has a concern, complaint, or issue with the other. Any attempt to discuss them becomes a free-for-all with no solutions and lots of anger, which results in distance and tattered feelings when it is over. With that in mind, it is helpful to set specific, basic ground rules to ensure you are heard, meaning your spouse takes in what you say. Voicing concerns without igniting a fight is possible with a few guidelines. I have five of them that will help.

FIVE GUIDELINES FOR SHARING CONCERNS, COMPLAINTS, OR ISSUES WITH YOUR SPOUSE

1. **Approach your spouse as a friend—that is, someone who accepts them rather than one who wants to change them.**

   In 1 Timothy 5:1–2, the apostle Paul says we should talk to people with respect and treat them as a friend when correction is the subject. Proverbs 15:1 also tells us that a gentle answer turns away wrath, but a harsh word stirs up anger. These are both true! When you start the conversation with humility, gentleness, compassion, and friendship, the possibility of success goes way up. However, starting the conversation with harshness, criticism, or excess emotion (see guideline four below), makes the chances of success next to zero. It goes without saying that talking about issues during a fight is a huge mistake, but people do it all the time. ("Well, if we are really going to talk about what is not working around here, what about the way you treat me when your mom is over?")

   People really can only hear correction when approached from a position of friendship, understanding, and acceptance. If we sense someone wants to change us or attack us who is not a friend, then our defenses go up and we resist whatever they are saying. Also, bigger issues may be met with resistance. If that happens, try addressing smaller matters first rather than one bigger issue that requires more from them.

2. **Figure out what problems in your marriage are perpetual versus solvable.**

   Did you know 70 percent of marriage problems are never-ending and will not be solved by any amount of talking? Yes, it would be better if they picked up their clothes but that may not ever happen. Yes, it would be a lot easier if they helped with certain chores but the chores you want them to do may be the most distasteful to them for some reason. Perpetual problems need to be understood, embraced, worked with or worked around. Sometimes it is just something a couple has to laugh about because it is just the way it is.

   I remember one couple had a room in their small house that they just wouldn't go into because they could not agree on how to clean it out. Things would get put in there but very few things came out. It stayed the "clutter room" for over ten years because the husband could not let the wife clean out the room the way she wanted to, and she could not let him clean out the room the way that he wanted to. Yes, it seems silly to us, but they stayed happily married, even with a room full of junk. They realized it was a perpetual, unsolvable problem at that time, so they embraced it instead of letting it divide them. Figure out which problems or irritations are perpetual and go from there.

3. **Share one concern at a time and wrap it in appreciation and gratitude.**

If we make a laundry list of the things that need to be dealt with and bring things up on that list to our spouse whenever we see them, they will grow really weary of seeing us after a while. It could feel to them like seeing us is always negative or problem-oriented, or they have another thing to correct or do. This is not what you want in a marriage.

We don't want a good spouse to become a nagging husband or a nagging wife. And we don't want to have our spouses feel like seeing us is negative. Instead, we want them to feel positive and encouraged whenever we walk in a room. Communicate how appreciative you are of all the good things your spouse is doing. If they always feel valued, appreciated, and thanked whenever you see them, they will want to see you more and do more for the wonderfully perceptive person you are.

There is a tendency with the efficient leader type to share lots of concerns or complaints at one time. "Let's just deal with it all at once while it's on my mind," they think. The problem is, this does not bring about the desired change. It lets the frustrated partner get things off their chest, but it doesn't improve the relationship or result in change. Practice one concern *per month* wrapped in acceptance and understanding.

Even though there are lots of things you might want them to change to make the relationship work best for both of you, refrain from giving them too much all at once. This is called *flooding,* and it will almost always cause the other person to disengage with you and make no changes at all. They will be like a stone wall which will not move. Men especially will shut down if too many things are rattled off at once. They just can't process them all to the point of making the change.

Think about it this way. If you limit the needed changes to one per month, that's twelve changes in a year. That's a lot of change! Prioritize what gets brought up. Only bring up the important ones that will really impact your relationship or your future in some significant way, because you don't get many of these per year.

I would also add that if you want to see someone change, then begin praising them for even the slightest movement in the right direction. The

Bible is constantly telling us to rejoice and be thankful and grateful because it is a powerful motivator for people. I can remember one store where I worked had a manager who wanted us to vacuum under the display cases. One of the first times I was vacuuming she stopped me and thanked me for vacuuming under the display cases and for doing such a good job. I don't know that I did vacuum under the cases before, but I did every time after that because I was praised for it.

In the same way, we can encourage our spouse to do new things by praising any movement in the new direction. Lead your spouse into a new behavior through praise instead of trying to scold them into it. When I first got married, I was not very good at pitching in to do household chores, but my wife went out of her way to praise me (practically throwing a party) every time I did something like take out the trash. I began to do much more around the house because of the praise.

I can also remember my wife saying that she did not like to read when we first got married, so I began praising her every time she read anything, and now she has both a master's and doctorate degrees, and she constantly reads all kinds of things. Think about what you want your spouse to do and praise them for moving in that direction instead of constantly criticizing them for not doing something or doing something wrong. Try this and you'll see it works.

4. **State your concern clearly and succinctly without emotion.**

Strong emotion is the toxin in this equation. When we wrap our concerns, issues, or difficulties in strong emotion, they may have more impact and gusto, but they also get the most push back. Separate the issue from the emotion and share what you are really talking about. We covered some of this with habit #11 about processing our toxic emotions. Express your request clearly and calmly, having decided ahead of time about why the concern bothers you and what change is needed. What is it that you want them to do and why? If they come back at you, stay calm and keep the emotional level low.

Rarely, if ever, does having a discussion wrapped in emotion work (anger, fear, tears, moodiness, depression, and so forth). Maybe it worked with your parents or your friends a few times, but it will not work long term with your spouse.

Emotions can be the drivers of all kinds of bad outcomes in marital discussions. It is not uncommon for a discussion to become a fight because one person is flooded with emotions due to what the other person is saying or doing. If you are going to get past fighting, you need to have a rule that allows people to calm down if they are flooded with emotion.

We had a rule in our home that we would wait two hours or two days to discuss things if one or both of us was highly emotional about the topic or issue. Some couples can work through their emotions much quicker. They can discuss it within twenty minutes or two hours, but don't be afraid to wait for two days. I think this is also why the Scripture says be angry but sin not. Take the time you need to calm down.

I find that many times when I allow myself to calm down, I can't even remember the reason I am upset in the first place. Some very interesting experiments have been done that show that if couples are interrupted when one or both parties are getting emotional and not allowed to start talking again until twenty minutes or more have passed that the whole interaction is changed for the positive.

Understand that one of you will be triggered emotionally by different things than the other. Give room for people to be emotional with the understanding that you will discuss these issues later or from a different angle so that progress is made in the relationship. Yes, you have to handle difficult issues like an adult, and adults learn how to manage their emotions and come to rational conclusions.

Also realize that 70 percent of the issues that might cause problems in a marriage, even good ones, have no resolution (see guideline two). You will not get every issue you want solved. You will have to work with a person who is completely different from you and who wants to ignore, solve, or continue in the problem. This is the joy of marriage. The best marriages learn to laugh about the issues that haven't been resolved. Just don't let negative or angry emotions flash out and damage a good and growing relationship. Let the other person have time to calm down.

5.   **Seek education about where the other person's behavior is coming from.**

Sometimes a person responds or promotes things in the relationship based on the way they were raised. All people have ways they act or do things that comes from their parents, upbringing, culture, or subculture. Is this the way their mom and dad did things? Are they just having a bad day? Is something else going on? Are they acting out of a pattern from their childhood? It doesn't make any sense to you necessarily, but it makes perfect sense to them because they were raised that way.

In marriage, there are certain topics that are constant sources of difficulty. A couple needs to decide together such things as:

How do we do mornings?

What do we do on the weekends?

What happens on holidays?

How will we train and discipline the children?

How should we handle our finances?

What is the connection (or lack of connection) to the extended family?

All of these and many others can generate complaints, concerns, or issues in marriage. Handle them one at a time, without emotion, realizing that it may just be the way that person was raised.

Decide with your spouse (conversation without emotion, exploring options and possibilities) what ground rules or rules of engagement you will employ whenever one of you has a concern, complaint, or issue about the other one. Change is possible if approached one-at-a-time in a clear, respectful, non-emotional, and understanding way. That's what couples who have ridiculously great marriages do.

Date Your Spouse Once a Week

Spouses need to have fun together. Too often, the hustle and bustle of life squeezes out the fun. But one of the crucial habits to include in a recipe for a ridiculously great marriage is to take your spouse on a fun date each week. It could be a big deal or something simple, like dinner and a movie, going to the lake with the family, or taking a hike. There are a thousand different things you can do. I remember when my father would take my mother square dancing on Tuesday nights. This said to my mother and to us kids that dad loved mom. They wanted to spend time together and it showed. He had fun with us too, like when he would take the family to the ice-skating rink on Fridays. But he and mom went dancing on Tuesday nights.

There will be times when the date isn't about doing the most exciting thing for one or both of you. The goal is not to have a great time personally. The goal is to have a great time with your spouse—together. What will allow that to happen? In a world of five hundred channels and a million pleasures, we can get very selfish and only want to do what is going to be maximally fun for us. But that type of thinking will often leave one spouse feeling very bored. The goal of a date is to explore each other's mind, will, emotions, personality, creativity, and new ideas.

What makes for a great date? I recommend asking questions. This allows you two to explore things you would not normally talk about. My wife and I were recently at a restaurant on our date, and I pulled out my phone to the Gottman Card Decks App. I selected the open-ended questions button, and we started answering them one by one. One of the answers I gave brought out a story about a cousin my wife had never heard about. We have known each other for over thirty years, but she had never heard me mention my cousin, Roger, even though I considered him to be one of my heroes in life. She was fascinated by my stories about him. We started to explore other friends and relatives who had made significant impact in our lives, which was very interesting and helpful to understand each other a little bit more. This is the goal I'm talking about.

Scripture doesn't specifically say we should have a date every week, but it does talk about pursuing our spouse regularly and constantly. The Song of Solomon in the Old Testament is a story of both romantic and erotic love. One of the famous lines is, "Draw me after you and let us run together!" (Song of Songs 1:4)

There is something very powerful and enjoyable about getting away from the normal routine to spend time with our spouse. It releases love and joy that are not released in the routines of life. Let me give you a picture from the Song of Songs 7:10–12 about the power of getting away by having a date or a short vacation.

I am my beloved's,

And his desire is for me.

Come, my beloved, let us go out into the country,

Let us spend the night in the villages.

Let us rise early and go to the vineyards;

Let us see whether the vine has budded,

And its blossoms have opened,

And whether the pomegranates have bloomed—

There I will give you my love.

Whenever I talk about or push this idea, I hear groans about the work or money it takes to date. A date or getaway doesn't have to be super creative or expensive; it just needs to be a time away from the usual routine where the two of you as a couple get a chance to have fun and talk on a deeper level. I highly recommend purchasing books full of questions so the conversation can go in new directions on your dates. There are great apps for your phone and whole books that have new date ideas. I also recommend creating a list of five to fifteen fun dates to pick from each week. I have found it is best to have the date be at the same time each week so it is not forgotten in the busyness of the schedule.

The date or getaway has to be an intentional part of your relationship. If you are not careful, you will go several weeks or months without getting away or spending alone time together. I have known many couples who refuse to leave their kids to take an overnight trip together. Trust me when I say your relationship is slipping during this time even though you don't know it. There are fewer little spider-web connections between you, like little kindnesses, little explorations, little acts of love, big gestures of faithfulness, and big actions of service. These are all necessary to keep love alive for decades; they go beyond when the kids are home. Find a trusted adult, like a grandparent, friend, or a neighbor to take the kids once in a while. It will do wonders for you *and* the kids.

The purpose of these dates and getaways are not just a prelude to sex; it is an opportunity to go out of your way to pursue your spouse's soul in an improved context. The aspect of emotional intimacy and desire to know the person is what makes the date richly rewarding. I often tell men that just like they enjoy fishing or hunting because they are chasing something, a date is similar. But instead of hunting a jack rabbit, they are hunting for meaning, understanding, wisdom, and emotional connection with their wife. It can be wonderfully fun, very helpful, and deeply rewarding.

Think of this time like putting money in a savings account you can draw out at a later time. Some teachers call this making a deposit into each other's emotional bank account. If you have enough positive reserves built up (which come with positive actions and kindnesses and good times spent together), then when something trying or difficult comes along (a negative action, lack of kindness, or separation), there are reserves to draw from. You don't want the account to be depleted where there is nothing left.

I have been with many couples who have gone through deep troubles and hard times. How good of friends they were before they got into those hard times often controlled how they got through them. Dating and time together as adults cements the relationship. Don't wait until you lose a job or have an illness or lose a loved one. Don't delay building your friendship with your spouse until the kids leave for college or you disagree strongly over something or a major change comes your way. It is often too late at that point. Develop as friends, week after week during the date.

Make sure your date nights are for fun things and not for business purposes. Don't let them become staff meetings. The point is to have separate staff meetings so your dates won't be all business. Try new things and explore new activities you both might like. My wife and I just took an archery class that was great fun. We have tried pottery classes, dance classes, lectures, exercise classes, bowling, golfing, bike riding, and many other things. Be careful of always going to dinner and a movie or watching TV. These can become ruts that are difficult to get out of. Every date may not be the most exciting thing in the world, but it creates bonds of friendship, fun, and understanding.

Dating and Getaway Components and Guidelines

Any good date has three components—food, activity, and conversation. A date can last anywhere from two to six hours, but again, every circumstance is different. Sometimes an hour is all you get when you have little ones, and that's okay! Getaways can start with an overnight out of town or even a local hotel down the road. Then you can build up to a weekend or a week-long vacation. Let's look at each of these components to maximize this time together.

1. **Food**

   My wife, Dana, is more of a food coinsurer and I am much more of a quantity food guy. So we have places that she really enjoys (they are more expensive), and places where I enjoy. The conversation is different at each. The questions and probing are different due to the elegance or casualness of the setting. Explore the culinary tastes for both of you; don't only insist on what you prefer.

   What kind of food places do you like?

   What kind of food places does your spouse prefer?

2. **Activity**

   When I counsel couples, I have them look through a list of common activities they might be interested in doing or trying. There are always new activities to try together you may have never considered before. In appendix 2, I have included a list of possible activities to talk about and explore together to open up new possibilities for dates (this list came from my book, *God's Radical Plan for Wives*). Before you turn there, think about the answers to the questions below. Take the answers into consideration as you glance over the list in appendix 2.

   What kind of activities does your spouse prefer?

   What kind of activities do you prefer?

3.   **Conversations to go deeper**

It's easy to talk about surface topics, like the weather, what you did today, and so forth, but the point of conversation during a date or getaway is to go deeper—to know your spouse at deeper levels than before. I tend to think in terms of the ten major relationships of life as that is where most of people's thoughts, issues, and difficulties lie. So during our dates, I ask my wife questions about these areas to see what she is thinking, what has happened in these areas that week, or what she is dreaming about in that area. I talked extensively about asking questions in habit #9—*Eat One Meal Together Every Day,* but the major relational categories I usually work through are God, self, marriage, family, work, church, money, friends, society, enemies.

Most of the time I don't get through all of these categories before the dinner is over or the movie has started or the activity interrupts. These areas change in each of our lives and are a tell-tale of what is happening in our soul. Everybody wants to talk about one of these areas with others. Your spouse especially.

When I'm talking with people, I regularly explore these topics and also account for their temperament impulses. This helps me relate to them better. Each person has different impulses that seem right to them based on their individual temperament. This is wonderful to explore if you can realize that there is no right or wrong answer. Each person just naturally wants to respond to a situation with their temperament impulse. These always come into play. They are always there. Knowing your spouse's temperament impulses helps you to know and anticipate their reactions and actions. You can explore with them the impulses of what certain situations and relationships bring up.

There are several temperament tests and quizzes I recommend, such as Myers Briggs, Ancient Temperaments (this is what I call it since it was originally discussed by Greek philosophers in 600 BC), *Love Languages* by Gary Chapman, and the *Enneagram.* Pick one of these to start discovering one another's temperament impulses. How do these various temperament tests actually affect the situations you have been going through or might go through? This is a great way to go deeper with your spouse.

The Point: Build Relational Wealth

I was prayerfully meditating on Scripture before I went on a little vacation with my wife, and the Lord strongly pointed out this passage in Proverbs about the critical importance of real wealth. Listen to what it says:

> *By wisdom a house is built,*
>
> *And by understanding it is established;*
>
> *And by knowledge the rooms are filled*
>
> *With all precious and pleasant riches. (Proverbs 24:3–4)*

Real wealth in Scripture is not monetary; it is relational. Are the people closest to you feeling like they are winning with the decisions and actions you are taking? Do the people you are tightly connected to see your understanding, wisdom, and knowledge? Do they feel built up in the relational aspect of life? It is this relational wealth that is the real wealth.

Think about this: If you have all the money in the world, but you have no one to share it with, then you are truly poor. To build a great life, you have to get along with your wife, your kids, your extended family, your near neighbors, and your remote neighbors. You have to embrace what we call an all-must-win point of view.

God was reminding me that my time away with my wife was crucial for the continued development of real wealth. This getaway was not just for me but for us. I get to explore her thoughts, her feelings, and her dreams. It is like mining for gold. In our day and age, we can be told to think that the only real wealth is job related or monetary but that is not wisdom. Wisdom is what action will allow everyone to win. Taking time to relate on dates, getaways, and vacations are a part of this wonderful thing called wisdom.

Date your spouse each week. Get away with them regularly. Go on vacation. This is the way to find more relational wealth and a ridiculously great marriage.

Conclusion

You have just read a book about the tools and essential habits of a ridiculously great marriage. I hope you will begin plugging these habits into your marriage one at a time over the next year or so. Use them and things will go so much better for you and your spouse. Ignore them at your own peril.

I advise that you don't try and insert them all in one week. Go slowly, one at a time. These have made such a huge difference in so many marriages, including mine. Even just adding one new habit will make a difference. I get great joy in hearing about couples who have inserted these absolutely essential habits into their marriages and how they are working. Please connect with me at www.info@ptlb.com to share your story about which habits worked for you.

As a review, I have put the table of contents here in the conclusion so you can work with the list of essential habits. Both husband and wife should look at the list, then answer the following questions. Talk about the differences between your answers and where you can put more energy to have a better marriage.

15 Essential Habits for Building a Ridiculously Great Marriage

Habit #1—Debrief Daily

Habit #2—Hold a Weekly Staff Meeting

Habit #3—Substitute Kindness for Sarcasm

Habit #4—Apologize When You've Blown It

Habit #5—Express Every Positive, Every Time

Habit #6—Seek Wisdom, Not Your Own Way

Habit #7—Pray Together Every Night

Habit #8—Schedule Regular Intimacy

Habit #9—Eat One Meal Together Every Day

Habit #10—Make Decisions Together

Habit #11—Learn to Forgive or Live in a Toxic Relationship

Habit #12—Align Your Expectations

Habit #13—Set Regular Budget Meetings

Habit #14—Stop Fighting, Start Learning and Discussing

Habit #15—Date Your Spouse Once a Week

My hope is that you won't just read this book and not do these things. I don't want you to be like the man who looked at himself in a mirror but forgot what he looked like after he stepped away from it. Pick one new habit and start there. Keep these in front of you and regularly refer to them. Memorize them.

I had a conversation with a young man at a conference recently. My wife and I had done premarital counseling for him and his fiancé some time ago using the material you just finished reading. I asked how he was doing in his marriage, and he said, "Great! The little habits make all the difference! If we skip a staff meeting or don't align our expectations, the relationship suffers."

There are many things you will need to do to make your marriage work. Every relationship is different. But the habits in this book are the most basic ones that benefit every marriage. When you add one on top of the other, they are powerful. Do not settle for an "okay" marriage when you can have a superior one. Find a way to develop a ridiculously great marriage and use these habits to change the very nature of your life. Soon, others will look at your relationship and want what you have.

Let me suggest that you print off or make a copy of these habits and put them on the refrigerator. Talk about which ones you want to insert into your marriage next. It is easy to delay this crucial step because you don't see it constantly. But if you put this list on the refrigerator, you will see it all the time. These are the secrets that you are looking for to improve your marriage. Start trying them. Even if there is only one of you trying...keep working toward these habits becoming a regular part of your marriage.

Acknowledgements

I am so grateful for so many people and influences that have come together in one of the most practical marriage books I have written.

I would be remiss if I did not acknowledge God's work in aiming me in the right direction for the material of this book. Scripture's insistence upon love, joy, peace, and patience in all of our dealings with people is paramount. God details the type of relationship we should have in marriage: one that is full of real love, friendship, respect, understanding, intimacy, and trust. With God's guidance, I have discovered that great marriages share these wonderful qualities through practicing particular habits that produce them.

I want to thank my wife for putting up with all the experimentation and development of the habits that we now find so dear. Dana, it truly is ridiculous how wonderful our marriage is. You are everything I could have hoped for and way more when I contemplated marriage. I am incredibly grateful for your patience, perseverance, prodding, and practical insights.

The book you hold in your hand is readable and complete because of the incredible efforts of my editor, Jennifer Edwards. Without her work in detangling my sentence structure and asking for more stories, the book would never exist in its present form. Jennifer, your insights and reworking of the material is brilliant. Thank you.

I want to thank Linné Garrett from 829 DESIGN for her layout of the pages and readability of the book. There is so much in the way the words are displayed that make them easy to consume.

Many thanks to Dave Eaton for his excellent feedback and cover ideas and design so that the book would draw in couples who want a ridiculous marriage.

I want to also thank all the excellent research that Dr. John Gottman has done in the area of marriage research. It has empirically confirmed the ideas and qualities that Scripture has directed for thousands of years. Long hours of watching, reading, and reflecting on Dr. Gottman's work is well worth the time.

I am indebted to Jud Boies for his excellent book on sexuality in marriage, *What's for Dessert?* Jud and his wife, Mary, are a wonderful couple who enjoy a ridiculously great marriage and have helped dozens of couples in their marital life.

Let me also thank Dr. Don Partridge for his insights and groundbreaking research on blended family structures. His book *Parent Wars: Dealing with an Ex to Build Emotionally Healthy Kids* is excellent.

Appendix 1

Ten Relationships in Life:
Questions to Ask Your Spouse

(HABIT #9)

God:

How is your life with God right now?

What is the last miraculous thing you have seen God do in your life?

How has God guided you through Scripture recently?

Which spiritual discipline is most powerful to you now?

> Confession, Holy Spirit, Bible Reading or Study, Prayer, Worship, Fellowship, Communion, Baptism, Fasting, Witnessing, Love, Giving

Self:

If life were ideal in five years, what would your life be like?

What are ten goals you are the most excited about?

How are you hoping to grow in your intellect and knowledge?

How are you hoping to harness, enjoy, and understand your emotions?

What are your physical goals?

How do you hope to maximize your spirit/soul in the coming year?

> Working with your conscience;
>
> Staying within your moral lines;
>
> Being creative in your ways;
>
> Connecting to God at a deeper level;

Understanding and embracing your
personality traits and quirks.

Marriage/Romance:

What in your opinion would enhance our romance?

What ways do you hope our marriage grows in the next year?

What romantic or relational elements can be added to our marriage?

What aspects of your inner-self do I not understand or know about?

What are the three most romantic evenings you can think of?

What is the difference between sexuality and romance?

What aspects of your personality or knowledge has not been explored?

Family:

What do I not know about your relatives?

Which relatives do I not know?

What do you want to know about my relatives?

What are your goals for our children and grandchildren?

What kind of parents/grandparents do we want to be?

Work/School:

What are you proud of at work/school?

If you could redesign work to suit your skills, what would be different?

What kind of contribution do you want to make to society through work?

What is the most interesting idea you have had at work in the last week?

Church:

What is the most interesting thing about church you can think of?

What are three problems with the church you attend?

How could church change to attract twice as many people?

Friends:

What are the three most significant aspect of good friends to you?

What new kind of friends do you wish you had in addition to the current friends you do have?

What would you like to try with a few trusted friends?

What problems do you have that required the help of friends to overcome?

Which friends have been there for you?

How have friends been there for you?

What are three activities you really want to do with friends?

Finances:

What have you learned about finances over your life?

What do you wish you knew about finances?

What do you wish you had never learned about money?

In the last week or month, what lesson are you learning about money?

What is one thing money can buy that you haven't purchased yet?

What is one thing money can't buy that you don't have yet?

What financial issue have you not addressed but you know you need to?

Society: community changes, politics, concerns

What troubles you societally that isn't getting a lot of press?

What issues in your city or region need to be addressed?

How do you want to be more involved in solving some of the problems?

What are you hoping your community wakes up and addresses?

What are three positive things about your city or region?

What are three negative things about your city or region?

If you could move to any city or region in the world, where would it be?

Who is your tribe geographically?

What is the most exciting current development in society?

What technological advancement is most exciting to you?

Enemies

Who would you say has been a consistent obstacle to you?

If you were to think back on those who talked down about you, who would those people be?

Which of the seven deadly sins are powerful temptations against you?

Pride, Envy, Anger, Lust, Sloth, Gluttony, Greed

Who would you say made you the angriest in your life?

If you were ever tempted to get involved in underworld activities, who was involved in tempting you?

Who tends to puff you up and make you feel like a big shot?

Appendix 2

Activities to Do Together

(HABIT #15)

Discuss the activities that you both enjoy or would be willing to try.

Building things	ATV 4-Wheeling	Pets
Crafts	Reading	Pinball
Racing	Watching TV	Air hockey
Working on cars	Movies	Table games
Sewing	Eating	Playing instruments
Crochet	Sleeping	Making music
Cricket	Tennis	Singing
Volleyball	Watching baseball	Parties
Football	Hiking	Baking
Basketball	Working out	Drawing
Spear fishing	Karate	Modeling
Swimming	Judo	Snorkeling
Snow skiing	Learning	Scuba
Cross-country skiing	Flying	Rollerblades
Tubing	Bike riding	Darts
Tobogganing	Jogging	Frisbee golf
Snowmobiling	Amusement parks	Archery
Motorcycles	Roller coasters	Flying planes

Sailing

Motor boating

Nature walks

RC Airplanes

Beach

Beach games

Horseback riding

Going out to eat

Fishing

Aerobics

Pottery

Antiquing

Boat shows

Home shows

RV Shows

Bowling

Roller hockey

Hang gliding

Skydiving

Museums

Cooking

Writing

Acting

Disabled ministries

Books on tape

Driving

Painting

Auto repair

White water rafting

Picnic games

Laser tag

Rock climbing

Canoeing

Kayaking

Historic sites

Conventions

Retreats

Speaking

Backpacking

Triathlon

Marathons

Soccer

Quilting

Racquetball

Golf

Talking

Waterskiing

Boating

Traveling

Photography

Developing pictures

Ice hockey

Ice skating

Camping

Running

Softball

Water parks

Horseshoes

Beach volleyball

Professional sports tickets

Spelunking

Mountain climbing

Gardening

Woodworking

Bird watching

Shopping for used books

Embroidery

Bow hunting

Rifle hunting

Investing

Calligraphy

Video games

Arcades

Shuffleboard

Table tennis

Windsurfing

Notes

HABIT #3

[1] Emily Esfahani Smith, "The Secret to Love Is Just Kindness," *The Atlantic*, June 12, 2014.

[2] Lawrence G. Lovasik, (1999). "The Hidden Power of Kindness: A Practical Handbook for Souls who Dare to Transform the World, One Deed at a Time," 189, Sophia Institute Press.

[3] John Gottman, PhD, and Nan Silver. *The Seven Principles for Making Marriage Work* (New York: Three Rivers Press, 1999), 26, 27.

[4] Drs. John and Julie Gottman, as cited in Emily Esfahani Smith's article, "The Secret to Love Is Just Kindness," *The Atlantic*, June 12, 2014.

[5] Ibid.

[6] Ibid.

[7] Shelly Gable, as cited in Emily Esfahani Smith's article, "The Secret to Love Is Just Kindness," *The Atlantic*, June 12, 2014.

HABIT #8

[1] Jud and Mary Bois, *What's for Dessert?* (coming 2020)

HABIT #9

[1] National Center on Addiction and Substance Abuse at Columbia University, CASA Columbia Study, https://www.centeronaddiction.org/addiction-research/reports/importance-of-family-dinners-2012

[2] "The Benefits of Eating Together for Children and Families," https://www.healthlinkbc.ca/healthy-eating/eating-together, last updated 2017.

HABIT #11

[1] "Forgiveness," Merriam-Webster's online dictionary, https://www.merriam-webster.com/dictionary/forgive, 2019.

[2] Dr. Donald R. Partridge, *Parent Wars: Dealing with an Ex to Raise Emotionally Healthy Kids* (Pleasanton: Pear Publishing, 2015).

[3] Gary Martin, The Phrase Finder, 2019, https://www.phrases.org.uk/meanings/there-but-for-the-grace-of-god.html.

ABOUT GIL STIEGLITZ

Dr. Gil Stieglitz is a prolific author, engaging speaker, and insightful pastor who has spent thousands of hours helping, coaching, and strengthening marriages. Gil has written over twenty-five books on marriage, parenting, soul development, and spiritual warfare, including top-seller *Becoming a Godly Husband*, *Marital Intelligence*, and *God's Radical Plan for Wives*. He speaks to thousands of people each year about the wonders of God's principles. Gil now serves as Discipleship Pastor at Bayside Church, a dynamic multi-site church near Sacramento, CA, and is on faculty with Principles To Live By, a nonprofit organization that helps people connect to God's principles in everyday life. He and his wife, Dana, enjoy a ridiculously delightful marriage in Northern California. For more information and to check out his other books, visit www.ptlb.com.

PRINCIPLES TO LIVE BY

Principles To Live By is a 501(c)3 organization that equips and empowers people, pastors, and churches. Our biblical resources, coaches, counselors, and teachers magnify God and ignite hope for better relationships, healthier Christians, thriving churches, and vibrant communities. PTLB hopes to reach hundreds and thousands of people with God's principles for transformational change. For more information, visit www.ptlb.com.

There Are Only Five Problems In Marriage.

★ ★ ★ ★ ★

Based on thousands of hours of marital counseling and study, Gil Stieglitz has witnessed the saving of hundreds of marriages. In *Marital Intelligence*, couples learn how to identify which of the five problems is at play in the relationship and how to get a handle on the myriad of issues, conflicts, and situations within the marriage.

1. Ignoring needs

2. Immature behaviors

3. Clashing temperaments

4. Competing relationships

5. Past baggage

Each problem is discussed in detail, along with antidotes, solutions, and self-tests making the material helpful and accessible for married or engaged couples, pastors, counselors, and marriage teachers. Useful for personal study, mentor-directed study, or as a guide for a class or lecture series, *Marital Intelligence* is the perfect tool to help restore marriages as God intended.

Available on Amazon.com, Christian Book Distributors, and wherever books are sold.

Published by BMH Publishing, Winona Lake, Indiana, 2019.

More Resources Available

www.PTLB.com

◆

BOOKS

Becoming a Godly Husband

Becoming Courageous

Breakfast with Solomon, Volumes 1 - 3

Breaking Satanic Bondage

Deep Happiness: Eight Secrets

Delighting in God

Delighting in Jesus

Developing a Christian Worldview

Getting God to Talk Back: Secrets of the Lord's Prayer

God's Radical Plan for Wives

God's Radical Plan for Wives Companion Bible Study

Going Deep in Prayer: Forty Days of In-Depth Prayer

Keeping Visitors

Leading a Thriving Ministry

Marital Intelligence: There Are Only Five Problems in Marriage
(Reprinted 2019, BMH Books)

Mission Possible: Winning the Battle over Temptation

Proverbs: Devotional Commentary, Volumes 1–2

Satan and the Origin of Evil

Secrets of God's Armor

Spiritual Disciplines of a C.H.R.I.S.T.I.A.N.

The Gift of Seeing Angels and Demons:
A Handbook for Discerners of Spirits

The Keys to Grapeness—Growing a Spirit-led Life

The Schemes of Satan

They Laughed When I Wrote Another Book about Prayer, Then They Read It

Touching the Face of God: Forty Days of Adoring God

Uniquely You: A Faith-Driven Journey to Your True Identity and Water
Walking, Giant-Slaying, History-Making Destiny

Weapons of Righteousness Study Guides

Why There Has to Be a Hell

◆

Online Video Courses through Udemy.com

Becoming a Godly Husband

Mission Possible: Winning the Battle over Temptation

The Keys to Grapeness—Growing a Spirit-led Life

Spiritual Disciplines of a C.H.R.I.S.T.I.A.N. (coming soon)

◆

Audio Files

Becoming a Godly Husband

Becoming a Godly Parent

Biblical Meditation: Keys of Transformation

Deep Happiness: Eight Secrets

Everyday Spiritual Warfare Series

God's Guide to Handling Money

Intensive Spiritual Warfare Series

Marital Intelligence: Battling for Your Marriage

Raising Your Leadership Level: Double Your Impact

Spiritual War Surrounding Money

Spiritual Warfare: Using the Weapons of God to Win Spiritual Battles

The Four Keys to a Great Family

The Ten Commandments

Weapons of Righteousness Series

Made in the USA
Monee, IL
21 January 2021